2.70

TORCH BIBLE COMMENTARIES

General Editors

THE REV. JOHN MARSH, D.PHIL.
Principal of Mansfield College, Oxford

THE REV. CANON ALAN RICHARDSON, D.D.
Professor of Christian Theology in the University of Nottingham

FOREWORD TO SERIES

The aim of this series of commentaries on books of the Bible is to provide the general reader with the soundest possible assistance in understanding the message of each book considered as a whole and as a part of the Bible.

The findings and views of modern critical scholarship on the text of the Bible have been taken fully into account; but we have asked the writers to remember that the Bible is more than a quarry for the practice of erudition; that it contains the message of the living God.

We hope that intelligent people of varying interests will find that these commentaries, while not ignoring the surface difficulties, are able to concentrate the mind on the essential Gospel contained in the various books of the Bible.

Volumes in the series include

THE EPISTLES OF
JOHN

Introduction and Commentary

by

NEIL ALEXANDER

Lecturer in the Department of Biblical Criticism
University of Aberdeen

THE MACMILLAN COMPANY

NEW YORK

FIRST PUBLISHED 1962
© SCM PRESS LTD 1962

PRINTED IN GREAT BRITAIN

To my Father
much beloved
*

III John 12

CONTENTS

THE FIRST EPISTLE OF JOHN

INTRODUCTION

PROLOGUE

1.1-4

GOD IS LIGHT

1.5–2.28

LIFE

THE SECOND AND THIRD EPISTLES OF JOHN

II JOHN

III JOHN

PREFACE

We possess in English two magnificent full-scale commentaries on the Epistles of John—those of A. E. Brooke and C. H. Dodd. Between them they treat virtually everything in the letters which calls for comment.

A writer on 'The Johannines' today can do little more than think these masters' thoughts after them. But he can perhaps spare the general reader the rigours of over-much technical discussion, and he can, in briefer compass, elucidate the message of the letters. To do this has been my aim.

Love of these letters was born in me, I would gratefully record, as a student of Professor G. H. C. Macgregor in Glasgow University. Something of that love, steadily deepened with the years and further study, has, it is hoped, flowed into the printed page.

My 'chief', Professor A. M. Hunter, whose volumes have lent such distinction to this series, has patiently encouraged me during the pains of a protracted literary 'first birth'. To him, and to my friend the Rev. George B. C. Sangster, D.S.C., B.D., whose experienced and careful proof-reading has been a valuable help, I render my warmest thanks.

My wife has for long lived in this production with me. Her preparation of the typescript has been only a fraction of her contribution to the book's completion. To her my debt is beyond measure.

NEIL ALEXANDER

King's College
Aberdeen
Easter 1961

SELECT BIBLIOGRAPHY

W. Barclay, *Daily Bible Readings: the Letters of John,*
St Andrew Press, 1958.

W. Barclay, *A New Testament Wordbook,* SCM Press,
1955.

A. E. Brooke, *The Johannine Epistles* (International Critical
Commentary), T. & T. Clark, 1912.

C. H. Dodd, *The Johannine Epistles* (Moffatt New Testament Commentary), Hodder and Stoughton, 1946.

B. S. Easton, 'The Letters of John', *The Abingdon Bible
Commentary,* Epworth Press, 1929.

G. G. Findlay, *Fellowship in the Life Eternal: an exposition of the Epistles of St John,* Hodder and Stoughton,
1909.

R. Law, *The Tests of Life: a study of the First Epistle of
St John,* T. & T. Clark, 1909.

A. Loisy, *Le quatrième Evangile, 2me edition refondue; les
Epîtres dites de Jean,* Paris, 1921.

J. A. Robertson, *The Gospel and Epistles of St John* (Bruce
Lectures), T. & T. Clark, 1919.

NOTE

Biblical quotations in the Commentary are normally from
the Authorised Version.

GENERAL INTRODUCTION

Away in the backwater of the New Testament, with Second Peter on one side and Jude on the other for companions, lie the Epistles of John. First John merits a position of greater distinction, and the minute Second and Third John could hardly be parted from it. The natural position to suggest is that immediately after the Fourth Gospel. Even if we did not think Gospel and Epistles were by the same hand, the juxtaposition would be reasonable. For one thing, the Fourth Gospel and the Epistles of John talk the same language. A distinctive Johannine terminology binds them together and, in this regard, sets them apart from the remainder of the New Testament. For another, the Epistles of John are full of reminiscences (some, almost certainly, deliberate) of the Fourth Gospel. They presuppose knowledge of that Gospel and, in the course of fulfilling their specific task, clarify, elaborate and apply much of its teaching.

All told, the Gospel of John and the Epistles belong together. In a sense the Epistles are 'born of' the Fourth Gospel. Quite properly the family might live together in the New Testament.

Many would object. The children, they would say, are feeble and lacking in personality, unworthy of their father's close company: John's Epistles on the heels of the Gospel would be 'a come-down', from the sublime to the trite, the brilliantly original to the banal and commonplace! How just is this? Certainly the Epistles contain hardly any idea not in the Gospel. Even 'God is light' and 'God is love', the First Epistle's two claims to novel phrase, express ideas of which, in embryo, the Gospel is full. Further, the First Epistle's subject-matter and style have a rather wearying

17   B

sameness throughout.[1] The Epistles do lack the Gospel's
rich stylistic variety and careful, studied construction. The
plan of the First Epistle (the others being too brief to make
judgment possible) is elusive. A few ideas recur again and
again. We may detect, perhaps, a *spiral* progression of argument. Yet even the slight ' spirality ' seems to be advanced
unconsciously and by almost fortuitous *verbal* links, as the
writer goes along.

By purely literary canons John's letters fall under the
above criticism.[2] But the New Testament is not artistic in
purpose. It is evangelical and hortatory. The Epistles of
John, written to meet readers' needs in an urgent situation,
are designed not to titillate minds or charm ears but win a
verdict for action! The true criterion of the quality of their
style and content is their suitability and adequacy for this
purpose. This test they pass with flying colours.

In I John, for example, the writer has certain things he
must get home to his readers. Their ' life ' is at stake, and
they are dear to him. So he says these things, simply, bluntly
and forcefully. Having said them, he does not dissipate their
effect by going on to treat less relevant matters. Instead, like
a good teacher (and a realistic preacher), he says them
again, and then again. They are not new truths, but that is
wisely of the writer's express purpose.[3] (After all, the
damage the First Epistle sought to rectify was, as we shall
see, caused by pseudo-Christian *novelties* in belief and practice.) Yet the writer, with these old original Gospel truths,
does something new. He takes them in their Fourth Gospel
form and re-presents them, often with a slight simplifying
variation, always with practical and ethical application. He

[1] Exactly every fifth verse in I John is a conditional sentence; and in
verses too numerous for pleasurable reading, the same truth is stated,
Psalms-like, twice, first positively then negatively.

[2] See I John 3.1-2, 20; 4.8, 16, 18, however, for verses of considerable
beauty in feeling and expression. Dodd concedes, too, the letter's
generally correct Greek and occasional pithy epigrams.

[3] I John 1.1-3; 2.7, 21.

pins down, as some contemporary Christians had to their convenience failed to do, in terms of day-to-day Christian obligation (in motive, spirit, action, relationships) the Fourth Gospel's soaring teaching.

John's letters do with great effectiveness what they set out to do, in style and content as wedded to their purpose as those of the Fourth Gospel to its different purpose. Their company would not shame their father! And their proximity to him, with their down-to-earth, repeatedly hammered-home ethical challenge, could not but be salutary still.

Whatever be the truth of their authorship and relation to the Fourth Gospel, the Johannine Epistles deserve and reward close study. They are found far from shallow, however simple they appear. If they are full of ethical ' do's ' and ' don'ts ' these proceed explicitly, as clearly as in any New Testament writings, from great Gospel proclamations. If they are intensely local in their original concern, focused narrowly upon well-defined situations in the Church of Asia at the close of the first century, we—for that very reason—recognise in them the thrilling pulse of the living, developing Church in the world as it did brave battle for its truth. And the situations themselves and the wisdom the writer brings to them we discover to be living problems and saving answers for the Christian Church today.

Behind this appraisal of the Epistles (as in the Introduction below (pp. 23-39 on I John and pp. 139-43 on II and III John) lie, of course, many issues of biblical criticism. For full discussion of these, and for the defence of conflicting viewpoints, we commend to the reader the excellent Introductions by A. E. Brooke (International Critical Commentary) and C. H. Dodd (Moffatt New Testament Commentary) on John's letters. Only minimal critical discussion is possible here.

THE FIRST EPISTLE
OF JOHN

INTRODUCTION

THE NATURE OF I JOHN

Is it really an 'Epistle'? Where are the greetings and personal names which mark the letter-form (e.g. as in Paul's letters)? Why not 'essay' or 'diatribe'? Because it is clearly written not to the Church at large but to a definite group of Christians (probably the congregations of one area) to whom the writer is in a longstanding relation of responsibility, authority and affection (2.1, 12, 18; 3.18): written, too, very much *ad hoc*, to meet an immediate need created by a critical situation (2.19) involving both writer and readers. It is a true letter, names or no names.

ITS AUTHORSHIP

A. *Relationship to the Author of the Fourth Gospel.* Tradition has unvaryingly declared the author of the Fourth Gospel to have written I John. This is still the majority view. A quick reading of I John will convince the reader—by its shared themes, language, verbal recollections of the Fourth Gospel—that common authorship is at least highly probable.

Close study, however, reveals certain points of difference between the two writings, in style, vocabulary, and theology. For Dodd these have sufficient force to make him deny common authorship of Gospel and Epistle. We believe, with Brooke, that the distinctions do not compel Dodd's conclusion. Here, in briefest compass, are the most important considerations on both sides.

23

Dodd finds significant difference between Fourth Gospel and First Epistle in their 'atmosphere'. The Epistle is, for him, 'less Hebraic and Jewish' (p. liii) and 'more free in its adoption of Hellenistic modes of thought and expression.' I John lacks, says Dodd, the Fourth Gospel's marked Semitic tinge and has only one Old Testament reference (3.12).[1] Words and forms such as 'seed' (3.9), 'chrism' (2.20, 27), 'we shall be like him' (3.2), 'God is light' (1.5), absent in the Gospel, are known commonplaces of Hellenistic mysticism. Even 'God is love' (4.8, 16), uniquely Christian conception though it is, is in Hellenistic form.

But there is counter-evidence. Many of the Epistle's terms, e.g. 'the devil sinneth from the beginning' (3.8), 'antichrist' (2.18), 'the blood' (1.7), 'propitiation' (or 'expiation') (2.2), 'purifieth' (3.3), 'the righteous' (2.1), 'this is the last hour' (2.18), are best, if not only, understood in the light of Judaism and an author whose mind 'is steeped in the thoughts of the Old Testament.'[2] Again, though Hellenistic words and forms may appear more boldly in the Epistle than in the Fourth Gospel, the Epistle is as uncompromisingly Hebraic-Christian as the Fourth Gospel in the explicit meaning which the author gives to these expressions.[3]

Further, in the Epistle these Hellenistic terms often carry invisible quotation marks! They are watchwords of the Hellenist heretics whom the author is combating and he uses them knowing they will be recognised as theirs. By choosing them, and by giving them sound, challenging Christian content, the author can, as it were, hoist the heretics with their own petards.

[1] II and III John have none.

[2] Brooke, p. 28.

[3] *Ibid.:* 'Though he has lived among Greeks and learned to express himself simply in their language and to some extent has made himself acquainted with Hellenic thought, he is really as much a stranger and a sojourner among them as his fathers were.'

If the atmospheres of Fourth Gospel and First Epistle differ, the difference is slighter than Dodd allows. It is sufficiently explained by the Evangelist's performance, in the Epistle, of a different task, in a different literary form.

Dodd finds also theological differences. (1) *The End.* Whereas in the Fourth Gospel the End is already fulfilled (Jesus has returned, in the promised Spirit come at Pentecost), in I John the End (e.g. ' when he shall appear ', 3.2) is imminent but still future. (2) *The Spirit.* In the Fourth Gospel the Spirit is personalised, as ' the abiding representative of Christ ', with Christ's authority and wide functions; in I John, says Dodd (p. 96), the Spirit is ' primarily the Spirit of prophecy—that is to say, an afflatus, or " inspiration " ' granted to some to confirm the truth of the Gospel as they preach or hear it. (3) *The Atonement.* The Fourth Gospel sees Christ's death as the climax of the redemptive revelation of God's love, and as the way through which Christ was ' lifted up ' in glory whence his eternal life can pour here and now into all who believe in him. I John, on the other hand, says Dodd, sees Christ's death in sacrificial terms, as ' expiation ' for our sins (1.7; 2.2).

But (1) both Gospel and Epistle have ' the spiritual idea of an abiding presence *and* the more popular conception of a day of judgment, a last day, a last hour ' (Brooke, p. xviii). In Epistle as well as Gospel, ' eternal life is a *present* possession and also an object of promise.' (2) In John 1.32-33; 4.23, ' Spirit ' is conceived very much as in I John. And (3) the Epistle's conception of Christ's death as expiatory ' is not absent from the Gospel ' (see John 1.29, 36: 11.50, 52).

The distinctions in theology are in fact merely differences in *stress.*

(Note that in each case the Epistle stresses the primitive *undeveloped* form of the Christian doctrine concerned. Why? Because the writer's need is to recall his readers from advanced notions to ' that which was from the beginning '

[1.1]. The Epistle's changed stress, from that of the Fourth Gospel, is thus deliberate, understandable and appropriate.)

There is no ample reason, we conclude, to cast aside the long-established tradition, and the impression of a first reading, that the Fourth Evangelist wrote I John. A disciple of the Fourth Evangelist, or an imitator, could have written the First Epistle,[1] but the traditional view has more to commend it and has still to be proved wrong. Till then, we take the author of Fourth Gospel and I John as one.

B. *The Identity of the Author.* But who is he? This obviously becomes now a question of: 'Who wrote the Fourth Gospel?' The evidence for judging this will be found fully gathered and wisely weighed in G. H. C. Macgregor's *The Gospel of John* (Moffatt NT Commentary). His conclusion, widely shared, is that the Fourth Evangelist, while possessing the tradition of John the Apostle, is not himself the Apostle John, but is most probably John the Elder (or Presbyter) of Ephesus in the province of Asia. I John, therefore (which tradition invariably associates with Ephesus), we regard as the work of John the Elder of Ephesus, one of that small revered 'group of teachers who formed a link between the apostles and the next generation' (Dodd, p. 155), whom Irenaeus calls, 'the Elders, disciples of the Apostles'. Note that II and III John (which there are no adequate grounds for ascribing to a different author) are openly written by 'the Elder' (II John 1; III John 1). See also Commentary on II John 1.

Both Fourth Gospel and I John show signs that the author was elderly. Irenaeus speaks of a John of Ephesus who lived on to Trajan's time (AD 98-118) who had been 'a disciple of the Lord', i.e. had followed Jesus in Palestine, AD 28-30. This aged John of Ephesus (whom he mistook for John the Apostle) might—just conceivably (no more)—

---

[1] We should then have expected, however, either a more exact copying of the Fourth Gospel in meaning as well as words, or a more radical departure from its characteristics than even Dodd finds.

be John the Elder, our author. If so, the author of Gospel and Epistle, in extreme youth, knew Jesus 'in the days of his flesh'.

THE DATE OF THE EPISTLE

Is Epistle or Gospel the earlier? Sometimes I John has been called a preliminary sketch of the Fourth Gospel's theology, the Epistle being shorter, simpler, and more primitive in its theological stresses. But 'many passages of the Epistle seem to need the help of the Gospel in order to become intelligible' (Brooke, p. xxii) and comparison of the Gospel and Epistle Prologues (clearly interconnected, reveals the Gospel as undoubtedly the original. 'The Epistle presents a summary, not a first sketch' (*ibid.*, p. xxvi).

The Fourth Gospel has for long been dated *c.* AD 95-105. More recently, since its independence of the Synoptic Gospels has been, with fair success, maintained, an earlier date, e.g. 85-95, has become possible. Even so, the heresy exposed in the Epistle and the established priority of the Gospel make us date the Epistle about AD 96.

ITS OCCASION AND PURPOSE

A. *The Occasion of the Epistle*. I John strongly suggests a letter its author was *driven* to write. From the Epistle's contents we can work back with confidence to the crisis which compelled it. The Elder's long work in the churches of the Roman province of Asia was in jeopardy. Some prominent church members, including teachers and prophets, had seceded from the main body. They had set themselves up, as, in fact, a rival Christian Church; in their own sight, the *only* Christian Church, with the only true doctrine and fellowship. They were continuing to succeed in attracting adherents. No doubt these included some, like themselves, from the Elder's congregations.

While secessions are always painful, not all have been harmful to the eventual welfare of the whole Church. But this secession, unchecked, could have killed Asian Christianity beyond foreseeable resurrection. John grasped this truth. Here was no mere slight to himself or blow to his life-work; no formal parting of the ways on personal or peripheral issues; here was Antichrist (I John 2.18, 22; cp. II John 7).

The outward expression of secession, radical enough, was a small matter, compared with its cause, the seceders' inward schism from Christianity itself. By belief and conduct, they had completely separated themselves from the Christian Gospel as handed down from the apostles (to John the Elder and others like him), and proclaimed and practised by the Asian Church under John's guidance for so many years. The situation, as acutely critical as any the New Testament records, called for John's quick, firm action. He penned the First Epistle.

B. *The Purpose of the Epistle.* John wrote for his own still faithful members. They were, we gather, rather diffident and weak, ' easily led '; by no means sure to see through the seceders' bogus claims; all too liable to ' go out ' after men so assured and successful. To match their need, John's letter has one comprehensive aim: to confirm the loyal in their possession of true Christianity and in assurance of their Christian standing. How does it do so? It recalls the readers again and again to truth that they, all of them, already have in the traditional Gospel and Commandment, and to the blessings they have all experienced in the Christian life. It reiterates the basic tests of sound Christian standing, e.g. walking in the light, love of one another, obedience to God's commands. It ends (5.13-21) with a series of grand affirmations assuring to them their present possession of all they need for victorious life in this world and the next.

The secession directly occasioned I John. In the letter the falsity of the seceders, and of their pretensions to true Christianity, is repeatedly demonstrated. The readers are put wise to the gravity of the seceders' perversions of Christian truth, and are armed to resist their specious appeal and defeat their propaganda. These 'destructive' passages are powerful, but it is important to note that the Epistle is not a polemic. The overall aim of the Epistle is (as stated above) constructive: the edifying of the loyal Church in Asia in sound belief and practice (in righteousness and love and truth) and in assurance of its fellowship in the true God, and of eternal life. All John writes is subsidiary and contributory to that positive purpose.

ITS STRUCTURE

The Prologue (1.1-4), recalling the Prologue of the Fourth Gospel, is clearly enough marked. Many also consider 5.14-21 as Epilogue. They note that 5.13 ('these things have I written unto you that believe . . . that ye may know that ye have eternal life') recalls John 20.31 ('these things are written that ye might believe . . . and that believing ye might have life . . .'). Just as (they rightly say) John 20.31 ends the Gospel proper, so I John 5.13 ends the letter's argument. What remains is Epilogue (cp. John 21). We agree that I John 5.13 deliberately recalls John 20.31. We judge 5.4b-21, however, to be the final section of the letter's argument, with its climax initiated by v. 13 and carried on right to v. 21. For us, no Epilogue.

What of the main body of the Epistle? Every commentator attempts an analysis. No two are identical. None is beyond criticism. Our attempt forms the Table of Contents (q.v.).

We find four main divisions:

> God is light (1.5–2.28)
> Life (2.29–4.6)
> God is love (4.7–5.4a)
> The True God (5.4b-21)

Each motif ('God is light', etc.) appears to control the thought of one division of the letter. Even so, the three other motifs, if temporarily subordinate, are not entirely dismissed. In fact, within the divisions 'God is light' and 'Life', righteousness (the dominant implication of 'light') love and truth are all related—in a remarkably repeated sequence—to 'light', then to 'life'. Thus:

> *God is light (1.5–2.28)*
>   Light implies Righteousness (1.5–2.2)
>   Light implies Love (2.3–2.17)
>   Light implies Truth (2.18–2.28)

> *Life (2.29–4.6)*
>   Life implies Righteousness (2.29–3.10)
>   Life implies Love (3.11–3.19a)
>   Life implies Truth (3.19–4.6)[1]

These divisions and subdivisions help us, at least, to see how John's letter moves; how in it Gospel truths are proclaimed, their ethical implications made clear, the seceders exposed and the faithful heartened.

Did John have any structural scheme in front of him as he wrote? His letter bears marks of being thought out pen in hand. Paragraphs are linked *verbally* rather than logically. That is, some single word in the last sentence of a paragraph is carried over to be developed in, and become the theme of,

[1] In the remaining divisions, 'God is love' (4.7–5.4a) and 'The True God' (5.4b-21), the internal pattern is somewhat similar but much less clear.

the next.[1] This bespeaks spontaneous writing, not systematic structure. Despite his spontaneity, however, the author never digresses for even a moment from the purpose of his writing.

THE FALSE TEACHING OPPOSED IN I JOHN

'Little children, keep yourselves from idols.' So ends I John. Strangely feeble words—but only at a first hearing. They are John's last solemn comprehensive warning to his readers to stand resolutely apart from all false teaching and practice, and to stand firm in the true Christianity his letter has proclaimed afresh. What are these 'idols' (or 'lies', as he also calls them) which attracted John's flock? As the Epistle combats the 'idols' it discloses them.

Identification is seriously disputed at one point only: namely that of the 'liars' who 'deny that Jesus is the Christ' (2.22; 5.1 [by implication]; cp.? also 4.15; 5.5 f.). Are they Jewish or Gentile Christians?

For Brooke, John's insistence on confession that 'Jesus is the Christ' points to their being Jewish Christians who, taunted by Jews without and haunted by resurgent doubts within, denied that Jesus was, after all, the Messiah.[2] We think Brooke mistaken, for the following reasons among others: (1) All other heretical teachings attacked in I John are recognisably Hellenistic and pagan—not Jewish—in origin. (2) Denial that Jesus is the Christ (2.22) expressed Hellenistic, just as much as Jewish, heresy. To Jews, of course, it meant: 'Jesus was not Israel's promised Messiah.' To first-century Hellenistic Christian heretics the same expression meant: 'The man Jesus was not inseparably,

---

[1] E.g. sin, 1.7-8; passing away/the last hour, 2.17-18; born of him/sons of God, 2.29–3.1; in truth/of the truth, 3.18-19; by the Spirit/the spirits, 3.24–4.1; our faith/he that believeth, 5.4-5.

[2] Brooke, pp. xli-xliii.

essentially, united to the Divine Christ.' (3) In this Epistle, the author could be said, almost, to be dedicated to making everything crystal clear! If he had intended to condemn two distinct groups (one of Jewish Christian apostates, the other, the main one, of Hellenistic Christian seceders), differentiation would surely have been unmistakably made. It is not so made, because, we judge, none was intended.

We believe the heresies attacked in I John to be all 'of a piece', and to spring from Hellenistic pagan 'lies' imported into Asian Christianity.

Can we (to change the figure) diagnose more particularly the Asian disease? Those who have 'caught' it say symptomatic things, such as[1]: 'Ethics don't matter' . . . 'we are *past* sinfulness' . . . 'we have not sinned' (1.6, 8, 10); 'we have superior knowledge' (2.20); 'we are above the moral law' . . . 'we have a special righteousness' (3.4, 7); 'Jesus is not the (Divine) Christ' . . . 'we need no Son to have the Father' (2.22-23); 'the Incarnation was not real' (4.3) . . . 'the (Divine) Christ was not crucified' (5.6a).

All these sayings point to Gnosticism; 4.3 points to Docetism; and 5.6a to Cerinthianism. We take Cerinthianism (which is a special brand of Docetism and Gnosticism) as the best one-word diagnosis of the I John heresy. Briefly now we explain in turn these terms[2]—Gnosticism, Docetism, Cerinthianism.

Gnosticism

'Spirit is inherently good: matter inherently evil.'[3] This simple proposition, for long an axiom of Greek philosophy, was the root idea from which the whole Hellenistic Gnostic system stemmed and flourished.

[1] Colloquialised, where necessary, to bring out their meaning. See Commentary on verses listed.

[2] Fuller accounts than are possible here are to be found in Barclay, *The Letters of John*, pp. 3-13; Brooke, pp. xliii-lii; Dodd, pp. xvi-xxi.

[3] Quite alien to Jewish thought. Cp. Gen. 1, esp. v. 31.

God, often spoken of as Eternal Light or Pure Reason, was entirely spirit, and therefore wholly good. The spiritual or rational part of man (explained as 'in some way a separated part of the supernal world, an effluence or radiation',[1] or 'seed', of the Spirit who is God) was also good. This good part of man could, in principle, associate with, and know, God. (Both belonged to the spiritual order.) But it was not free to do so. It was imprisoned in the material world and the inherently evil flesh of a man's body. The mass of men (*psychikoi*) were thus doomed to live in evil and darkness, ignorant of God and the world of light. But for some men (*pneumatikoi*) freedom was possible. By elaborate secret rites (revealed to, and through, true Gnostics only), visions and other modes of mystical communion, they could transcend their 'evil' flesh and worldly environment. Their freed spirits then rose to the heavenly world of spirit where they had immediate knowledge (*gnosis*) of God. Indeed, they said they had union with, and identity with, the Divine Spirit.

Serious dangers in Gnosticism are at once apparent: three in particular.

1. *Spiritual snobbery and arrogant exclusivism.* 'We special people, we only, know God. The *hoi polloi*, earthbound slaves of "too, too solid flesh", are beneath the possibility of knowing God—and beneath our contempt.'

2. *Self-authenticating religious experience the all-sufficient and supreme good.* 'Through our rites we "know"[2] God—and "see" and "love" and "abide in" him. Nobody can challenge that. We know we know God. And this mystical contemplation of the Eternal Spirit—this, *per se*, is life in the light, the good life and the true.'

3. *Ethical indifference.* 'In union with God we have, *ipso*

---

[1] Dodd, p. xvii.
[2] Gnostics, as well as Christians, used the terms in quotation marks.

facto, spiritual perfection. Thanks to our *gnosis*, we are *above* sin. The sinful body and material world no longer control us. Their welfare no longer concerns us. What we do with them, what, indeed, we *do* at all, is irrelevant. Spirit is all, and we are spiritual. Have not we known God and seen him? Are not we one with him? '

The Gnostic character of many of the heretical sayings implied in I John and listed above will now be clear.[1] Such sayings as ' Jesus is not the Christ ' (2.22), ' the Incarnation was not real ' (4.3), ' the Christ was not crucified ' (5.6a), also derive from the spirit/matter (or soul/body) dualism at the root of Gnosticism, but we give these errors distinctive names: Docetism and Cerinthianism. Both have to do with the Person of Jesus Christ.

Docetism

When Christianity spread into the Greek world, the pagan Gnostic welcomed it. He saw in it a *gnosis*—a way of knowing God—apparently like his own.[2] But he despised it as inferior. Christianity clung to what he called outworn myths. One above all the Gnostic dismissed as puerile, that ' Jesus the Christ was come in the flesh ' (4.3). By that Christians meant that God, without ceasing to be divine, ' became flesh ', and was born, lived, suffered and died, in the truly human Jesus of Nazareth. To a Gnostic this belief was benighted and, indeed, blasphemous. Never could the true God,[3] the Eternal Spirit (or ' the Christ ', i.e. for Gnostics, 'a spiritual emanation from the true God ') be

[1] John's answer to these Gnostic ' dangers '—taken in order—is to stress (1) the meaning of Christian fellowship, (2) the need to test knowledge of God by its fruits, (3) the plain Gospel commands to do righteous deeds and love the brethren.

[2] In terminology and rite: e.g. salvation, rebirth, baptism.

[3] Logic forced Gnostics to deny that the true God had ever created the world, so evil. They invented a creator-God called the ' demiurge ', hostile to the true God.

believed to have permitted his absolute goodness to be defiled by real involvement in the evil material world and bodily flesh!

For many Christians this Gnostic challenge was too powerful. They became Gnostic Christians, committed to grave Christological heresy. Jesus Christ, they said, only seemed to be man, and to have a truly human body. He was really spirit, phantom, all the time.[1] Only in appearance did the Divine Christ come in the flesh (4.3). No Gnostic Christian could avoid some such form of *Docetism* (from *dokein*, 'seem'), the heresy that the human life of Jesus Christ, the Divine Son of God, was one big pretence, that 'the Incarnation was not real'.

Cerinthianism

The Epistle alludes (e.g. 5.6a) to Cerinthianism, a special brand of Docetism, so named after Cerinthus, an Ephesian Gnostic whom, in the oft-quoted tale set in the baths at Ephesus, John vigorously denounced.[2] Cerinthus accepted as real the human life of *Jesus,* but not of Jesus Christ. He separated 'Jesus' from the 'Christ', denying that Jesus was (in permanent relation of essential unity with) the Christ (2.22).

The human Jesus, he argued, was born like any other baby. Christ (the Divine Power or Spirit, the Saviour) only descended upon Jesus at Baptism and left him just before the Crucifixion. The cry of dereliction, 'My God, my God, why hast thou forsaken me?', was the cry of the human Jesus newly bereft of the Christ power.[3] Thus Jesus, the ordinary human, was born and suffered and was crucified,

---

[1] In the heretical Acts of John it is said that when Jesus walked he never left any footprint upon the ground.

[2] Eusebius, *Eccl. Hist.* IV 14.6, credits John with the words: 'Let us flee lest even the bath-house fall, because Cerinthus the enemy of truth is within.'

[3] The Apocryphal *Gospel of Peter,* c. 130, actually alters Mark 15.34 from 'My God, my God' to 'my power, my power.'

but in these painful human experiences the Divine Christ, being pure Spirit, had no part. It appears to be this view that John combats (5.6a) when he declares, with great emphasis, 'This is he that came by water and by blood, even Jesus Christ; not by water only' (an allusion to the Baptism) 'but by water and blood' (the Baptism and the Crucifixion). (See Commentary *ad loc.*)

Docetism at large evacuated our Lord's whole Incarnate experience of its Christian worth. Cerinthianism (with its Redeemer-Christ untouched by birth or suffering or death, only temporarily and superficially connected with Jesus of Nazareth) made of orthodox *Atonement* doctrine in particular so great a travesty as to be its complete denial.

John was justified in calling the Asian heretics antichrists. Their heresies, disguised as more enlightened Christian faith, attacked the very heart of Christian faith itself. For us, as for John, that 'heart' is this: that when the Eternal Divine Word came he became *flesh*—true human flesh—not in 'seeming' but in reality; and yet that he was ever as he had been—the *Word*, Eternal, Divine.

Be it in Bethlehem's manger or by Jordan's bank or in the agony of Gethsemane and Golgotha, we gaze upon him who is alike one with man and one with God; perfectly qualified (as only one such could be) to accomplish our Atonement; always the truly human, yet never *merely* human, Jesus; always Jesus Christ the Divine Son of God.

How, we may ask, could Cerinthian-Docetic-Gnostics beguile John's members into heresy and secession? The following four factors may partly explain.

(1) The sincere pagan Gnostic (of the ascetic type) was in many ways an admirable character: a man, it might seem, to emulate. To Christians, in the context of corrupt pagan society, the 'good' Gnostic (over-individualistic in piety, indifferent to his brother, falsely other-worldly though he

was, even at the best) would shine with 'a clear, pure light'.[1]

(2) There were many obvious similarities between Gnosticism and Christianity. The least intelligent and the least instructed of John's members would be drawn to Gnosticism—a strong movement which, at the close of the first century, enjoyed a social respect denied to Christianity—persuaded that 'Christianity and Gnosticism were saying the same thing'. They crossed the Gnostic line, innocents abroad in heresy-land.

(3) Some of the brighter of John's members, impatient of tradition and genuinely eager for the Church's onward missionary march, would find Gnosticism most attractive. It sold itself to them as the enlightened, civilised man's religion. It offered to do for traditional Christianity, by 'gnosticisation', what these Christians believed needed: to bring it slap up to date, in line with modern thought. 'Let Christianity drop its old-fashioned notions (e.g. of real Incarnation) and fuse with Gnosticism! Thus purified and made intellectually respectable and mature, Christianity (i.e. *Gnostic* Christianity) could win the sophisticated world of our day!' So, not improbably, the teachers and prophets of the I John secession may have imagined. (In actual fact, of course, in embracing Gnosticism, they surrendered the Gospel.)

(4) The Fourth Gospel itself—its teaching carelessly and wilfully misread, its genius unappreciated—may have been mistaken as pro-Gnostic.[2] Its Prologue terminology; its dualisms such as 'dark and light', 'love and hate', 'God

---

[1] The Gnostic *Corpus Hermeticum* (1st-3rd Cent.) probably reflects Christian thought. This allowed, the beauty and nobility of many Gnostic sayings therein still suggests the justice of our point above. See citations in R. Bultmann, *Primitive Christianity in its Contemporary Setting*, Eng. trs., Thames & Hudson, 1956, and C. K. Barrett, *The New Testament Background: Selected Documents*, SPCK, 1956.

[2] The Fourth Gospel, slow to be received in some orthodox Christian circles, was in fact welcomed by some heretical Christian groups.

and the world'; its stress on 'knowing' and 'rebirth'; its
esoteric teaching and mystical air, were all familiar and
appealing features to those brought up amid Hellenistic
cults and philosophy. John probably employed them, as
such, of set purpose, to serve his evangelistic aim.

Yet (aided by the Dead Sea Scrolls) we recognise these
features *as they appear in John* to be, in origin, Jewish.
There was what might almost be termed a *Jewish* Gnosticism, before Christianity was born. It is this Jewish dual-
istic language which John uses—and with Jewish-Christian
meaning. (N.B. This Jewish dualism was never metaphysical, always ethical. It accepted nothing of the spirit/
matter division of the Greek world. Its division was between
good and evil in one spiritual/material world under one
good God.) Nonetheless, these Johannine dualisms quoted
above were phrases actually employed by Gnostics too.
Superficially, John and the Gnostics *were* saying the same
thing.

Some Asian Christians (such as in (2) above), nurtured on
the Fourth Gospel (or on similar teaching, before its publi-
cation), may, misled by the Hellenistic-sounding language,
have missed its points of radical divergence from pagan
Gnosticism.

Others, such as those in (3) above, may have had their
appetite for modernity whetted by the Fourth Gospel's own
brilliant attempt to re-state for Gentiles the primitive Gospel
in terms they knew. 'Why not go further?', they may have
asked. These missed the essence of that Gospel's achieve-
ment—viz. its knowledge of just where to stop in re-state-
ment of the primitive Gospel. (Take the Prologue. It uses
many terms common to Gnostics, yet it is wholly Christian,
never Gnostic. What indeed could be more true to the
primitive Gospel, more starkly *anti*-Gnostic, *anti*-Docetic,
than 'the Word was made flesh and dwelt among us'?
And all through the Gospel the essential Christian scandal
of a genuine historical revelation of God in a passionful

human life and death is quite uncompromised by John's daring terminology. Hellenistically dressed in appearance—intentionally so—it remains at heart the old simple Palestinian Gospel.) To avoid, as it does, any distortion of the traditional Gospel in 'translation' called for the genius of a John. Failing to appreciate this truth, and reckless of the dangers which John had averted by going so far, no further, the leading seceders may have rushed ahead. They found themselves at once in Gnosticism: out of John's Church and, to his mind, out of Christianity.

The Fourth Gospel, then, may—ironically enough—have actually encouraged some of its readers to embrace doctrinal errors which its author abhorred!

We conjecture that when the Elder came to write I John he was appalled not simply by the secession and the heresy but by the awareness that, through weak or wilful woolly-mindedness, many members of the Church had misconstrued his own teaching, his very own Gospel, as giving them licence to 'go Gnostic'. Hence I John's repeated hammering at teachings he had already given them: the frequent taking of Fourth Gospel ideas and the making of their meaning plain beyond conceivable mistake. Hence the acute sense the Epistle creates of John 'telling the story simply as to a little child'. It *is* the 'old old story', the Palestinian story in its Fourth Gospel translation. It *is* 'simply' told. It had to be. For not only through bonds of fatherly affection for them, but also with dismayed experience of their slender understanding, he wrote to, and about, those who were as 'little children'.

COMMENTARY

PROLOGUE

1.1-4

No personal greetings herald I John: instead a four-verse Prologue of great moment and power. Why 'Prologue'? These verses (one single sentence in Greek) do preface the whole letter; and they recall the Prologue to the Fourth Gospel. Such reminiscence, even more striking in Greek[1], must be meant to bring the readers at once into the thought-world of the familiar Fourth Gospel, which, through the Epistle, John purposes they should understand and practise more soundly.

OUR DECLARATION

1.1-3a

The complicated opening sentence needs special care.

A. *Concerning the Gospel.* Omit in the meantime v. 2, the parenthesis. Verses 1 and 3a mean: *We declare,* (v. 3a) *concerning the word of life* (v. 1 OF THE WORD OF LIFE), *that which originally belongs to it* (v. 1 THAT WHICH WAS FROM THE BEGINNING[2]) *and is attested by eyewitnesses* (v. 1 WHICH WE HAVE HEARD . . . SEEN . . . HANDLED). 'Concerning'

---

[1] Brooke, pp. xxv-xxvi.

[2] Beginning of creation? or of the Christian dispensation and preaching? Probably, despite John 1.1 and Gen. 1.1, the latter. So also in I John 2.7, 24; 3.11.

40

rather than 'OF' preserves the clear Greek distinction here between direct (THAT WHICH . . .) and indirect (OF THE WORD . . .) object of DECLARE WE. The word of life is not itself what is declared: it is the area of the declaration's concern.

Note that we have taken away the AV's capital W from WORD OF LIFE, for we understand 'word of life' to be 'the Gospel'. Moffatt, on the other hand, takes Word in its Fourth Gospel Prologue sense = Christ the Logos, the Personal Word of God, making OF LIFE correspond to the Fourth Gospel's 'in him was life' (John 1.4a). Attractive! But, throughout the Epistle, though John strongly recalls his Gospel, he rarely *repeats*: and Fourth Gospel terms are regularly less technical in meaning when used in the Epistle. So, probably, 'the "logos" of life' is here simply 'the word which reveals and brings life', 'the revelation of life' (Westcott), i.e. the Gospel. An interpretation confirmed by the closest New Testament parallels to John's conjunction of 'word' and 'life' (Phil. 2.16; Acts 5.20; John 6.68).

B. *Eternal life* (v. 2). Throughout this letter John loves to define terms. Here WORD OF LIFE (v. 1) touches off the definition of LIFE. Not just life in general, any chance notion of life! He means that life, eternal, WHICH WAS WITH THE FATHER and was seen by eyewitnesses in Jesus Christ Incarnate. The word of life is the word of *this* life! '(Eternal) life' stands high among the Epistle's keywords. It is one of its first words (1.2), almost its last (5.20), and implicit throughout. '*This* life we declare to you.'

WE . . . SHEW (v. 2) and DECLARE WE (v. 3a) are identical in Greek. Hence we have twin declarations: ETERNAL LIFE (v. 2) and THAT WHICH . . . WE HAVE SEEN AND HEARD (v. 3a, taking up v. 1). So vv. 1-3a mean substantially: *We declare, concerning the Gospel, the eternal life seen in Christ Incarnate and in so doing we are declaring what originally belongs to the Gospel and is attested by eyewitnesses.*

C. *We bear witness* (v. 2). THE LIFE WAS MANIFESTED,

AND WE HAVE SEEN IT, AND BEAR WITNESS. John declares
eternal life thus, by bearing witness to Christ, in whom it
was made visible and knowable. The Greek word *martyrein*
(bear witness to), a favourite with John,[1] has a legal flavour
as in English. One who bears witness solemnly guarantees
the truth of what he has seen and heard at first hand and
knows. The Twelve were commissioned by Jesus (John
15.27) 'to bear witness',[2] because they had been with him
'from the beginning'—hearing, seeing and handling Christ
himself and the Kingdom's words and works. They could
say 'I was there!' 'I saw!' 'I heard!' They *could* 'bear
witness'.

WE HAVE SEEN . . . AND BEAR WITNESS, then, is apt if
WE means an apostle, writing for all the apostles. But the
author is unlikely to be an apostle. It is still apt if John
the Elder, our suggested author, was during AD 28-30, in
early youth, 'a disciple of the Lord'. (That is, WE means
'I, John the Elder, and my fellow-survivors who saw and
followed the Incarnate Jesus in the days of his flesh.') Just
possibly true.[3] Even so, we must go deeper. We find[4] that
John uses WE of no closed group of eyewitnesses but of all
sound Christians of any date! They *all*, rather WE all, are
eyewitnesses of the Incarnate Life and entitled to bear witness. Can this be squared with the first-hand-ness inherent
in BEAR WITNESS?

(*a*) By the idea of spiritual vision, insight? The physical
emphasis in v. 1 (OUR EYES, OUR HANDS) and the Epistle's
later *anti*-mysticism rule that out.

(*b*) By the idea of Christian solidarity? Yes. Through
oneness in Christian faith and fellowship we today—like
John in AD 96—can speak of, indeed do *possess*, the apostles'
experience and witness as our own.

---

[1] Ten times in his Epistles: thirty-three in his Gospel.
[2] Cp. Luke 24.48; Acts 2.32; 3.15; 1.8.
[3] See Introduction, pp. 26 f.
[4] Cp. I John 4.13-14; Dodd, pp. 9-16.

Is the notion really alien to us? A burgher of Rutherglen today says without artificiality: 'We received our Royal Charter in AD 1126.' Not long ago a C.S.M. of the Royal Leicestershire Regiment declared on television: 'By 1823 we had been 18 years in India. . . .' To belong to Rutherglen or the Leicesters is to be bound up in, and appropriate to oneself, their past, present and future.

Far stronger was this sense of solidarity in ancient societies, especially in Israel, created and bound by divine calling and covenant. To the Jew, his own and his people's experience were almost indistinguishable—even with five hundred years between them—as Amos (2.10: 'I brought you up from . . . Egypt') shows. Christian solidarity is still stronger. The New Testament Christian always knows himself incorporated in the New Israel, with even more to belong to, more to possess (through Messiah come, redemption won and new covenant established) than had the Jew.

What the first-century Christian felt profoundly is profoundly true. Every Christian is more than an individual. Qua Christian, he belongs to the whole Church: no less he possesses the Church's total historical experience and, in particular, the experience of its formative events. So John, with the first-hand-ness of Christian solidarity, aptly writes and means: THE LIFE WAS MANIFESTED, AND WE (we of the Christian Church) HAVE—literally—SEEN IT, AND we, (I, the author, writing as and for the Church) BEAR WITNESS (to the life we have seen).

N.B. The YOU in vv. 2, 3 and 4 (John's readers) are not over against, but included in, the WE. YOU and WE alike are the Church. The only significant contrast to WE in the letter is 'those outside', 'the world' (when used to mean non-Christian forces of pagan society, as in I John 3.1, 13; 4.4-6; 5.4, 19).

OUR FELLOWSHIP

1.3b, 4

3b. . . . that ye also may have (continue to have, realise fully) **fellowship with us**

The purpose of ' our declaration '. Those addressed are faithful but timid and in danger of following a bad example. I John 2.19 explains. Some prominent members had gone out from the Church, openly and outwardly breaking fellowship. Why? Despite appearances, 'they were not of us': they—radically—had never had FELLOWSHIP WITH US. Thus warned, John sees the faithful's greatest need: a strengthened hold on this FELLOWSHIP.

Clearly FELLOWSHIP for John is a profound word for a rich reality. With us it means often a mere surface association, for convenience and pleasure, of people unconcerned in each other save in some one part-time (social, cultural, recreational) interest: e.g., debates, dancing, darts, Diaghilev, even divinity (as an intellectual pursuit). Even Church fellowship may be shallowly misconceived, as only a kind of ' jolly-good-fellow-ship '! John's Greek word, *koinōnia*,[1] means (at root) sharing, participation, partnership, joint ownership. The AV translates it by ' communion ' in I Cor. 10.16, of ' communal participation in ' Christ's Blood and Body. Our ' calling ' by God is (I Cor. 1.9) ' into *koinōnia* ', ' into participation in ' his Son. These are fair indications of the importance of *koinōnia* (or fellowship) and the deep personal involvement which, rightly used, it denotes. Most illuminating, however, are the great Church ' parables ' of the Vine and Branches (John 15.1-6) and Members and Body of Christ (I Cor. 12). They describe a relationship (branches-Vine, branch-branch, members-Head, member-

---

[1] This word rewards detailed study. See W. Barclay, *A New Testament Word Book.*

member) that is organic: inward and essential for life, sustenance, fruitfulness and performance of function. It is a sharing by Christians, with each other, of one single life, that life which they all possess, and only[1] possess, through sharing in the (Spirit-imparted) life of Christ. This is John's FELLOWSHIP: an involvement in Christ and each other so close and vital that life itself depends upon it, that this fellowship *is* our life! No less do we rightly mean when we speak of 'the Christian community' or 'belonging to the Church'.

fellowship with us
Probably, 'fellowship with Christ such as we Church members have.'

Truly our fellowship ('our' emphatic) is with the Father and with his Son Jesus Christ
Another definition. The object of the Church's 'participation' is quite specific. An odd use of Greek particles (which the AV renders TRULY) conveys awe and wonder: 'Ours is nothing less than a sharing in God and his Son!'

and with his Son
Denied or ignored by the heretics (2.23; 5.12), but all-important to John. Only through the Son has the Father been revealed and his life made communicable to men.

4. that your joy may be full
Better reading, 'our joy . . .' Undoubted reminiscence of John 15.11 (cp. John 16.24). The key is *koinōnia*. The whole Church suffers if any members (YOU) have incomplete participation. (Cp. I Cor. 12.26.) If YOU act on the letter's advice (THESE THINGS), then WE (you, I the writer,

---

[1] 'Without me' (i.e. severed from me, the Vine) 'ye can do nothing' (John 15.5): you are lifeless, fruitless branches.

and the whole Church) will harvest joy in full measure!
Thus the Prologue ends.

GOD IS LIGHT

1.5–2.28

LIGHT IMPLIES RIGHTEOUSNESS

1.5–2.2

Essay I: GOD IS LIGHT (1.5)

Background. This precise phrase, unique in the New Testament, has a mystical sound. Did John take it over from
Greek philosophy and current Hellenistic cults? Platonists,
Zoroastrians and Gnostics did employ much light-imagery,
quite naturally associating light with good and with God.
Philo, the contemporary Jewish Platonist, wrote the very
words 'God is light' (*De Somniis* 1.75). Doubtless John
knew the phrase as used in philosophy; probably, too, as a
maxim of the Gnostic seceders.

But ample and, we believe, primary, stimulus for its
Christian use was in the Old Testament and John's own
Gospel. Cp. Pss. 4.6; 27.1 (which prompted Philo's use);
43.3; 36.9: 'in thy light shall we see light'; Isa. 60.20;
John 1.9; 8.12: 'I am the light of the world: he that fol-
loweth me . . . shall have the light of life.' Further, John
expressly asserts that this very message, God is light, *we
have heard of him* (Jesus): i.e. that it is not borrowed but
belongs (in substance at least) to Christ's teaching.[1]

---

[1] Even the Synoptics contain 'light'-teaching conducive to 'God is
light'. Cp. Luke 11.34-36; Matt. 5.8, 48.

Form. It was, nonetheless, a bold expression for Jew or Christian. When Philo dared it his next words almost retracted it. The Jew in him, insistent on God's personality and transcendence, feared its apparent[1] equation of God with an abstract quality or a created object. Though John would also hesitate, it served his practical purpose to use this phrase he could accept which was also current among the seceders. They would say: 'Good! John says it too!' Then John could the more effectively expose their radical divergence in interpretation.

Meaning. Two main meanings John gives to 'God is light' (the motif of 1.5–2.28). (1) God's essential nature is *to reveal himself* (and hence reveal, including 'show up' in contrast, all else).[2] (2) God's essential nature is *moral perfection.* In this latter meaning the phrase is immediately employed.

It is because in God 'there is no darkness at all' (v. 5) in the sense of 'God is goodness through and through' that evil-doers (walkers in darkness) cannot claim fellowship with him.

Whereas, for Gnostics, 'God is light' is merely a mystical notion to 'get lost in', for John it immediately spells God's absolute ethical demand upon men. If God is perfect in righteousness, sharing in him must mean sharing in his righteousness, by doing righteous deeds.

Thus John's sound Christian common sense delivers 'God is light' from the dangers of Hellenism and heresy: it leads him to present, forthrightly, the permanent challenge of the Christian truth the phrase enshrines.

THE SECEDERS' CANT EXPOSED

1.6, 8, 10

This challenging tone ideally suits the letter's subsidiary

[1] *Only* apparent: so in John. God is not named '*the light*'.
[2] So used in 2.3 ff. See pp. 55, 65.

purpose: to expose the heretics' false claims. What claims? From John's denunciations in at least four passages (1.6, 8, 10; 2.4-11, 2.22-23a and 3.4-9) we can infer them.

The first passage implies and deals with three bogus claims:

> (1) 'Ethics don't matter' (v. 6)
> (2) 'We are "past" sinfulness' (v. 8)
> (3) 'We have not sinned' (v. 10)

(Verses 7 and 9, along with the other purely positive teaching of 1.5–2.2, are treated under 2.1, 2.)

We best capture the spirit of vv. 6, 8 and 10 (and like passages) by making explicit their implicit dialogue between John and the Seceders.

(1) *'Ethics don't matter'* (v. 6)

Seceders: We have fellowship with God: wonderful communion with him!

John: All very fine, but what about ethics?

S.: Ethics? What have they to do with the case?

J.: Everything! You agree God is light? What, then, are you doing, you who profess to have fellowship with God, living in darkness? That's what your wickedness *is*—darkness: complete exclusion from the unmarred light of goodness which is in God. You have no part or lot with God. To claim otherwise is a deliberate lie. Your failure to practise goodness proves that.

Timelessly fair comment upon all whose religious experience, to judge from their daily conduct, contains no moral imperative at all.

6. walk

i.e. live. The Greek term, like its underlying Hebrew, emphasises conduct. So in the archaic English 'daily walk and conversation'.

. . . in darkness

Their fellowship with God cannot be believed, since light and darkness exclude each other. Cp. perfect love and fear (4.18): liberty (Spirit, faith) and law (Gal. 5.1, 2, 18). Paul asks (II Cor. 6.14): 'What fellowship has light with darkness?'

we . . . do not the truth

No phrase could better show John's staunchly Hebraic and Christian outlook. For him THE TRUTH is not something simply to know, but something, known, to DO. Does 'doing the truth' sound odd? Not when we note that in LXX *alētheia* (truth) translates the Hebrew *emeth*, 'reliability, faithfulness': first in God, then in man. In God, the truth is revealed, supremely in God Incarnate in Christ, as 'faithfulness in goodness'. In man, whose true life mirrors God's nature, 'the truth' is his like fidelity, in 'the highest of which he is capable in conduct and feeling as well as . . . word and thought.'[1] Hence, to DO . . . THE TRUTH is, as John 3.20 f. shows conclusively, to 'practise goodness'. (On 'truth' etc. see Commentary also at 2.18-21; 3.18; Life implies Truth [3.19-4.6] and The True God [5.4b-21]). Sometimes elsewhere John's use of 'truth' and 'true' suggests a more nearly, though never quite, Hellenist (Platonist) meaning, 'the ultimately Real'. Not at all here. 'DOING the truth' would be an intolerable expression to any Greek mind.

(2) 'We are " past " sinfulness' (v. 8)

Seceders: What talk is this of 'cleansing from sinfulness in all its forms' (v.7)? Not for us! You are addressing enlightened Christians. Our enlightenment *means* our spiritual perfection. Our sinfulness is a thing of the past: as a power in us it died long ago.

---

[1] Brooke, p. 14.

John: How you deceive yourselves! Stop your make-believe! You are anything but perfect. Own up to your day-to-day experience of sin's continuing activity in you! Until you do, you are 'strangers to the truth' (NEB).

Such Gnostics are perennial. It is an irony that they often mistake John himself—his *caveat* here conveniently forgotten—as saying (e.g. in 3.6, 9) 'Christian therefore, *ipso facto*, morally perfect: "above" sin!' *O si sic veritas!* Paul (Phil. 3.12-14) rings true to Christian experience: 'not as though I had already attained, either were already perfect . . . I count not myself to have apprehended: but this one thing I do . . . I press forward.'

8. We have no sin

Some,[1] swayed by John 9.41; 15. 22, 24; 19.11, interpret as 'we are not guilty'. But Fourth Gospel parallels need not determine First Epistle meanings. Further: SIN (*hamartia*, singular) in v. 8, only three Greek words after SIN (again *hamartia*) in v. 7 and clearly prompted by it, most naturally shares its meaning of sinfulness, sin, principle of sin. So translate: 'We are "past" (or "beyond the sphere of") sinfulness altogether.'

(3) *'We have not sinned'* (v. 10)

Seceders: We ask you again: why talk to us of 'cleansing' (v. 9)? *We* need no cleansing, no forgiveness. These are for people burdened by their past misdeeds. Not so are we. We have committed no sins. We've done nothing to forgive.
John: Blasphemy! Not content with lying—consciously (v. 6) or involuntarily (v. 8)—now you make *God* a liar! '*All* have sinned'[2]—as you well know. Besides, for what do you think Jesus Christ came, died and rose? Precisely to deal with sins

[1] E.g. Moffatt; R. Law, *Tests of Life*, p. 130.

[2] John need not have in mind any specific Old Testament Scripture (e.g. Pss. 14.3 ; 53.3), but simply the whole Old Testament's view of man's condition as 'fallen'.

(1.7b, 9; 2.2), ours and the whole world's! You say 'you
have not sinned'? So God has been radically wrong in his
diagnosis of the human situation? He has provided an
atonement man does not need? You are flatly denying the
Gospel's relevance. Why, it is not in you at all!

So stands condemned every attempt to fashion, even
preach, a Christianity silent about sins. It encourages, now
as then, our natural proneness to flee from admission of
actual sins. And it still falsifies the Gospel which is, after
all, 'for sinners only'.

10. We have not sinned

The Greek perfect tense implies a continuous present
state resulting from past action. (? 'We have no burden or
history of sinful deeds.') Specific sins, sinful acts, are probably meant (as in v. 9), not 'sinfulness' as in vv. 7 f.

6, 8, 10. To sum up: the seceders are fully convinced of one
quite *un*apostolic doctrine, the Doctrine of the Special Person, as applied to themselves. In this they are typical
Gnostic Christians: spiritual snobs, holding themselves—
whatever 'ordinary' Christians may be like—*above* considerations of ethics, *above* the power of sinfulness, *above*
the commission (and confession) of sins. Their claim to
be so rests entirely on their claim to specially advanced
illumination through mystical communion with God. John's
reply is that their 'illumination' is bogus, their 'mystical
communion' invalid. It must be. It has led them to attitudes
and practices which repudiate the Gospel at every turn.
Their cant is exposed.

But even while picking up seceders' phrases to condemn
their views, John keeps his loyal flock in mind. Especially
for them the positive teaching of the remaining verses of this
section is given.

1.5, 7, 9; 2.1-2. *Don't sin, but if you do—there is forgiveness.*

John declares to them (by GOD IS LIGHT, v. 5) the absolute moral perfection of God. Fellowship with him means not mysticism but moral congruence with him. If they have that —walking by grace where God is by nature—then they have fellowship with each other (v. 7a), in virtue of their fellowship with God. They 'share together a common life' (NEB).

They know that to be true, but John grasps that its sting for the heretics (v. 6), reaching the faithful also, may lead them to say: 'We know we are far from perfect: we walk in darkness ourselves at times, sincerely as we love the light. Are we too excluded from God?' 'By no means irremediably,' says John: 'Christ's shed life-blood removes your sin (v. 7b) and restores you to the light.'

If they honestly admit their sin, God is 'such as to be counted on to be just' (FAITHFUL AND JUST: v. 9a) in his dealings with them, whatever their sins: God will forgive and cleanse.

2.1. John is suddenly alarmed. The readers might mis-interpret him (especially in 1.10) to mean: 'Everybody sins, so why worry about sins? Besides, God forgives!' So, very emphatically, with the address MY LITTLE (Moffatt: 'dear') CHILDREN, of a father-in-God's affectionate authority, he says: THESE THINGS WRITE I UNTO YOU, THAT YE SIN NOT. 'The very purpose of this letter is to warn you: *don't* sin! But, should you sin, don't despair. There is forgiveness.'

On two grounds already John has given this assurance: (*a*) Christ's death brought cleansing (1.7b); and (*b*) the Father initiates and seals that cleansing (1.9). Now he adds: (*c*) Christ exalted still engages on our behalf (2.1 f.). He is our ADVOCATE WITH THE FATHER. Remember who he is: JESUS CHRIST THE RIGHTEOUS. In that very title is triple certainty of his successful advocacy! 'As true man (Jesus), he can state the case for men with absolute knowledge and real sympathy. As God's anointed messenger to men (Christ), he is naturally fitted for the task and acceptable to him before whom he pleads. As righteous, he can enter the Presence from which all sin excludes' (Brooke, p. 27). And, most cogent ground of all: (*d*) our advocate, so defined, is himself (HE emphatic in AND HE IS, v. 2) the efficacious means[1] whereby God can forgive OUR SINS. John is arrested by his word OUR. Can he end there? As the grandeur of redemption's range 'comes over' him, he goes on: 'NOT . . . OURS ONLY, BUT . . . THE SINS OF THE WHOLE WORLD! To the world, even though largely hostile, Christ is given as its priceless means of forgiveness.

1.7b. the blood of Jesus Christ his Son cleanseth us from all sin

Probably (cp. John 1.29, 36) from John's tradition of the apostolic preaching, like 'Christ died for our sins' (I Cor. 15.3) for Paul. The idea of the cleansing power of (shed) BLOOD, life offered in death, has roots in Lev. 17.11 and underlies the whole Jewish sacrificial system.

cleanseth

Literally, 'makes pure'. 'Removes sin' rather than 'cancels guilt'.

9. he is faithful and just to forgive

God the Father can be counted on to be JUST: therefore he will forgive. The readers would understand, but we may not. How will God's unfailing justice help? Is not his *relaxed* justice our only hope of forgiveness? Not at all. In the New Testament God's justice (or righteousness) means not just an attribute but an activity of God, whereby 'the right is asserted in the deliverance of man from the power of evil.'[2] The Atonement which wrought this deliverance

[1] AV, propitiation. See pp. 54 f.
[2] See Dodd's classic notes on Rom. 1.16 f.; 3.21-26: *Romans* (MNTC), pp. 8-12, 48-61.

springs from the justice of God. It is thus his justice which makes possible, and issues in, his mercy and forgiveness. 'A just God, *therefore* a Saviour' (Isa. 45.21).

9. he . . . to cleanse us from all unrighteousness

Virtually the same formula is applied to the Father as, in v. 7, to (the blood of) Christ. The cleansing work of Christ is not only offered to God but is *of* God. It is God's purpose: God's work. Cp. 'I have finished the work which thou gavest me to do' (John 17.4). Acts 2.22-39, John 3.16 and Rom. 5.8 all stress Atonement as the Father's work.

2.1. an advocate

Greek, *paraclētos*. Primarily, but not exclusively, a law-court word. Wider, then, than the English 'advocate'—still our best translation—it signifies 'a friend called to the caller's assistance'.

Whereas the Fourth Gospel instances[1] (two with the legal, two the non-legal sense) all refer to the Holy Spirit, here in I John—the only other New Testament reference—the ADVOCATE is CHRIST. We believe this to be one of the theological simplifications characteristic of the First Epistle and well-suited to its clarifying purpose. 'Christ our advocate' has definition which 'the Spirit our advocate' might dangerously lack for some Christians. Note that emphasis on *Christ* as Exalted Intercessor is no idea peculiar to I John. See Matt. 10.32; Heb. 2.17b; 7.25; Rom. 8.34.

2. propitiation

Better, 'means of forgiveness' or (RSV) 'expiation'. One of Dodd's most helpful researches has been into the meaning of this word (Greek, *hilasmos*) and its cognates.[2] Only the findings can here be stated. Whereas in pagan Greek the verb underlying *hilasmos* mostly means 'placate', 'pro-

[1] John 14.16, 26; 15.26; 16.7-8.
[2] See Dodd, pp. 25-27; also his *Romans*, pp. 54-55.

pitiate', some angry offended person, usually a god, in the Greek Old Testament this usage is 'practically unknown where God is the object.' The sense there is of 'performing an act whereby guilt or defilement is removed'.

Ritual defilement is expiated by the performance (by the defiled man or another on his behalf) of a specific ritual act. If defilement is moral—so later Hebrew thought perceived —the required 'expiation' is beyond man to offer. God alone, the only good, can expiate man's moral defilement. Hence (in Hebrew and Christian use), God can be subject of the verb 'expiate'. 'God expiates' means 'God removes man's moral defilement' (the barrier separating man from God), i.e., in effect, 'God *forgives*'. Christ is the *hilasmos* (or *hilastērion*, Rom. 3.25), the *means* whereby God expiates our sins: 'the means of our forgiveness'.

LIGHT IMPLIES LOVE

2.3-17

The theme 'God is light' continues. Now its sense is not so much 'God is moral perfection' as 'God reveals himself'. (See p. 47.) THE TRUE LIGHT NOW SHINETH (v. 8), for example, means: 'This is the era of God's perfect self-revelation.' It has been made in the Person and teaching of Jesus Christ, and is summed up in one sublime word: love. If we really know and abide in God, his revealed love for us makes love for him and our brethren our only fit response. 'The man who says he abides in God is obliged to live in the same way in which Christ lived' (v. 6): the way of love. Moreover, he *commanded* us to love (v. 7).

3. *To know God, obey him*

'Here is the test by which we can make sure that we know him: do we keep his commands?' (NEB). John is no

legalist yet fourteen times in this letter he writes COMMAND-
MENT. There is no contradiction. John recognised only one
commandment, the command to love (vv. 7, 8a)—the one
quite beyond legal measurement or enforcement. Even so,
it is absolutely binding on Christians.

THE SECEDERS' CANT EXPOSED

2.4-11

John's Gnostic opponents seem to have been saying
otherwise, by practice if not by word.

(1) *'Obedience is irrelevant'* (v. 4)

Seceders: We know God all right. This ' obedience ' of yours
doesn't enter into knowing God, or loving him (which is a
matter of mystical experience).

John: Nonsense! Knowledge of God, whenever authentic,
carries divine claim with it. Our God's claim is in his known
command. Obey you must. That is what it means to know
God, and to love him truly (v. 5).[1]

(2) *'We need not love our brother'* (v. 9)

Seceders: We are in the light (of knowledge of God). We love
him. What difference does it make whether we love or hate
our *brother*?

John: A world of difference! Since the substance of God's
command is ' love your brother ', hatred shows inevitably—
in the same moment—your disobedience, your darkness, your
ignorance of God. If you're in the light at all (vv. 9 f.), you
simply cannot hate your brother, for ' the light ' *means* love.
Make no mistake: love your brother, or stand condemned
as still stumbling about in the Christless dark! (v. 11).

---

[1] ' But whoever keeps his word ' (commandment), ' truly in him love for
God has been made perfect ' (RSV).

5. love of God

Better, the Christian's ' love *for* God '.

has been made perfect

Fulfilled, brought to fruition. The contrast is not with some imperfect kind of love but with unrealised, unactualised—almost ' deedless '—love. Such love (to John) is not love at all.

7-8. No new commandment . . . but an old commandment . . . again (RSV, 'yet') a new commandment

This is difficult. What is FROM THE BEGINNING? Why is the command OLD yet NEW? It is best taken thus. ' No NEW command am I inventing and issuing: I am recalling one OLD and familiar. You had it from the beginning of your Christian experience, for it is part of the original Gospel (John 13.34). (Indeed any Jewish Christians among you had it also from childhood, in Judaism, since the basis of the COMMANDMENT intended is Lev. 19.18.) '

Yet it *is* NEW. Why? (1) Jesus himself called it NEW and made it new, by defining our commanded brotherly love by his own love for us (John 13.34: ' Love one another as I have loved you '). (2) It is NEW also because it is *the* commandment of the new age (the fulfilment-time, the end-time) which Christ's mission inaugurated. The word NEW, *kainos*, often means new in kind as well as time. Most notably it describes features of the age to come, e.g. new covenant (I Cor. 11.25; Heb. 8.8-13; 9.15), new teaching (Mark 1.27), new man (Eph. 2.15; 4.24), new creation (Gal. 6.15). (See on v. 8b for ' the age to come '.) So, here and in John 13.34, the COMMANDMENT is NEW since it belongs to, and obtains in, and is realised in, the era of ' the last days '. And for John these days are here, since Christ's coming.

which thing is true in him and in you

The WHICH THING (neuter in Greek) is not the command

itself but, probably, its newness. Its newness (in sense (2) above) has been made actual (IS TRUE) in Christ and in YOU (the Christian fellowship). NEB beautifully simplifies by transposing this clause to follow the AV sentence end. Then the WHICH THING becomes the shining of THE TRUE LIGHT. 'Christ has made this true, and it is true in your own experience.'

8. Because the darkness is past, and the true light now shineth

Why the commandment is NEW. RSV, more exact than AV here, has: 'because the darkness' (of ignorance of God) 'is passing away and the true light' (of God's self-revelation, now come in Christ) 'is already shining.' The old age has begun to go but has not yet vanished. The new age has already dawned, but now is its dawn, not yet its noon-day. Cp. I Cor. 10.11. It calls Christians those 'upon whom the ends of the world are come'. The 'ends' are the overlapping ends of the two ages into which the Jews divided the whole of time. The Christian era is the winding-up of 'this present age' and the start of the 'age to come'.

Verse 8b is most important. Of its truth John is utterly convinced. This conviction provides him with his perspective and us with the key to many features throughout the letter. *The true light is already shining.* This means that the true God is known: eternal life is to be had now; the law of brotherly love, like Christ's, operates and is realised in the new order now begun. *The darkness is passing away.* The darkness of the old order is still very evident, in the godless world and its desires, e.g. 'the lust of the flesh, and the lust of the eyes and the pride of life' (v. 16). But they are already doomed, with the darkness their sphere; they have no future (v. 17).

Here to stay—and exclusively so—are the new age realities, e.g. the light, love, and life now revealed and communicated by Christ, and the new age *man.* 'He who does the will of God' (i.e., in John's terms, the Christian who has 'life' and who walks in the 'light' and 'loves God and his brother also') 'abides for ever' (v. 17).

This is the New Testament perspective, hard to share in our own day. Evil in man and in the world is strongly ranged and rampant. Often its power seems paramount: that of light, life and love so insignificant. Yet for John appearances were at least as daunting. The Christian communities were socially outcast and materially resourceless, often bedevilled by heresies and unruly, unworthy members. Outside was the massed hostile, often persecuting, might of Rome, and of the non-Christian religions which it tolerated and encouraged. Where was any sign, in AD 96, that the old order was decisively defeated and passing away? Where was visible evidence that the true light had already dawned, and that its perfect day was assured? How often John must have been told to be *realistic*!

But faith still declares John to be the true realist, in looking not on the outward appearance but upon the heart of history. That 'heart' remains the—to faith—incomparably decisive event of the ministry, death and resurrection of Jesus Christ.

9. He that saith he is in the light and hateth his brother is in darkness even until now

Hatred belongs to the realms of darkness and the world: love alone to the light. To hate your brother shows where despite all your profession you still belong.

10. and there is none occasion of stumbling (*skandalon*) in him

i.e. in the man himself: no internal stumbling-block of contradictory light profession and dark practice. But the parallelism in vv. 10 f. may favour Moffatt (followed by RSV) who takes IN HIM as 'in it' i.e. in the light. 'In the light there is no pitfall.' Cp. John 11.9 f.

11. Knoweth not whither he goeth

Cp. John 12.35. The blinding effect of hatred and dark-ness-dwelling upon the man of 'the world'. He is just groping in the blackout. Christless man, it appears, has *always* lacked direction.

12-14. *The Blessings of the Light*

These verses effectively precede John's emphatic ban (vv. 15-17) on any compromise with the world. They give the best of reasons why yielding should be unthinkable and unnecessary. We might paraphrase thus:

> 'Why do you suppose I write in these terms? Because you are Christian brethren, alive to the " true light that is already shining ". Count your blessings! Your sins are forgiven for Christ's sake. You know the Eternal God. You have con-quered the evil one.[1] You are strong, in your new-age possessions through Christ. Then possess your possessions and be strong! Have no dalliance with the world (vv. 15-16)! '

Three matters merit note in these verses.

(1) The accomplished work of Christ is neatly presented in its major aspects: revelation of God, forgiveness of sins, victory over the world (cp. John 1.18,29; 12.31; 16.33).

(2) John argues here (and throughout the letter) from the present Christian knowledge and privilege he assumes in his readers. His principle is explicit in 2.21: 'I write to you, not because you do not know the truth, but because you know it' (RSV). He writes not to inform but to remind. Then he summons the readers to act with consistency upon their refreshed knowledge.

(3) These verses are 'in a rhetorical, almost poetical, form, consisting of two sequences of three aphorisms. . . . The three aphorisms in each sequence are addressed respec-

[1] Vv. 13 f. Whatever our view, the devil was personal to John as to Jesus. Cp. John 12.31.

tively to *children, fathers,* and *young men*' (Dodd). The letter as a whole so lacks literary artifice that its presence here suggests John's special anxiety at this point to grip all his readers' attention. The threefold classification into age groups, LITTLE CHILDREN . . . FATHERS . . . YOUNG MEN etc., some find more subtly significant. We doubt if it is more than rhetoric, homiletically useful. 'All the privileges mentioned,' Dodd says well, 'belong to all Christians, but emphasis and variety of expression are secured by distributing them into groups.'

I write . . . I write . . . I write . . . I write . . . I have written . . . I have written

Better texts yield I WRITE for the first sequence of three, I HAVE WRITTEN for the whole second sequence. The change from present to past is simply an attempt, by use of the epistolary aorist,[1] to add variety. It introduces no significant difference in meaning from the present; it is just another feature of these stylised verses.

15-17. *Don't love the world: love the Father—you will abide forever.*

John uses WORLD in two quite different senses according to context; as (1) all creation, especially all humanity; (2) human society apart from God, the totality of the forces ranged against Christ and his Kingdom: 'the godless world'.[2] So he can say both 'God so loved the world . . .' (John 3.16) and 'Don't love the world' (I John 2.15); both 'Jesus Christ . . . is the means of forgiveness . . . for the sins of the whole world' (2.2; cp. 4.14) and 'if any man love the world, love for the Father is not in him' (2.15b). Sense (2) is intended throughout vv. 15-17.

Note the stark contrast John makes between Christian and WORLD. Christian, and Christian society, are character-

[1] In which the Greek past tense used is accurate by the time the letter is being read.

[2] NEB's translation of *kosmos,* where appropriate.

ised by forgiveness of sins, knowledge of God, victory over
the evil one (vv. 12-14); by love of the Father and doing his
will; by abiding for ever (vv. 15-17). Pagan society (which is
what the WORLD in sense (2) virtually means) is 'in the
power of the evil one' (5.19; cp. 2.13 f.) and is characterised
by 'sensuality, materialism and self-glorification' (Dodd on
v. 16)—and 'passing away' (v. 17).

John's message is:

> 'Be adamant in resistance to the world's appeal. If you are
> not—if in practice you love the world and set your heart on
> what it stands for—then you simply don't love the Father.
> You can't do both: these "loves" are mutually exclusive
> (cp. Matt. 6.24). Besides, remember the days of pagan society
> and its sensual attitudes are numbered! Love them and you
> will go down with them. But why should you? The future—
> eternity indeed—already lies with you who do love the Father
> and do his will.'

John has New Testament company in his attitude to the
world, e.g. James 1.27; 4.4; II Cor. 6.14-18. To his credit he
neither rejects the world in the sense of 'the physical and
material order' (like the Gnostics), nor demands flight from
sinful society (into some Christian Qumran-type community). Yet is not John's attitude dangerously negative?
It says in effect: 'Pagan society is "going hang". Let it go.
Keep clear of its taint. Keep to yourselves and keep clean
and safe.' Where is John's missionary spirit? Is he remem-
bering that pagan society is part of the world 'God so
loved'? Possibly not.

John was probably actuated here by three beliefs he held
true.[1] (1) It was so late—Doomsday only an hour away
(v. 18); (2) Pagan society was so corrupt—no Christian
could touch it without being corrupted;[2] (3) Pagan influence

---

[1] See also on II John 10-11. The Prohibition.

[2] See William Barclay, *Expository Times*, LXXI, 9 (June 1960), pp.
280-284, for an admirable analysis of the iniquities of the time.

had already done serious damage to the Church—in 'those who had gone out' (v. 19) and in the compromising spirit in the membership at large.

(1) *It was so late.* He is just about to say: 'This is the last hour' (v. 18). Of course it is *always* 'late' in the Christian era of 'these last days'. But John in AD 96 believed the days had run out, that it was 11 p.m. on Doomsday Eve. Time left for Christians only to ensure that they themselves should be found blameless in the day of the Lord—tomorrow morning!

(2) *Pagan society was so corrupt.* Even when Tacitus, Juvenal, Seneca, etc., are taken with several grains of salt, their records of Graeco-Roman society of the time reveal its utter degradation. Vicious corruption, extending to every aspect of life, was the pagan world's hall-mark. (Cp. Rom. 1.21-32; I Cor. 10.20-21; II Cor. 6.14-18.) Honesty, chastity, humanity, unpretentious living, were contemned. Lust and avarice, bribery, fantastic luxury, frantic search for new pleasures, callous recklessness of human life and dignity (e.g. in gladiatorial butcheries, exposure of children, unbridled sexual vice) were socially accepted: almost 'normal'!

So degraded was John's world (and so small the Christian community) that we are probably thinking not only Dodd's but John's thought after him in saying: 'The Church had no choice. It could bear its witness only by separation from pagan society' (Dodd, p. 46). The pitch of first-century paganism was too widespread and too mortally adhesive to be deliberately touched by Christians.

(3) *Pagan influence had already done much serious damage.* Verse 19, just ahead, tells of some who went out from the Church in Asia. Explicitly in 4.1 they are said to have gone out 'into the world'. Their false teaching, we know, resulted from their 'mixing it' with the world's ideas. Nothing in the letter suggests that the seceders became grossly immoral, but by a man of John's either-or mind their fatal love of the world's *ideas* would be construed as only part of their comprehensive 'love of the world and the things that are in the world'. The vehemence of the veto in

vv. 15-17 may spring from thought of what worldly association had done to the seceders, and—through them—to the
Church.

   More certainly, the general membership of the churches
in John's care seem to have been inclining to tolerate and
adopt worldly attitudes and practices. John is alarmed by
this careless compromise. He knows that, in the crisis of the
times, it could prove fatal to the Asian Church. He writes
as incisively as he does to nip this danger in the bud.

John's position is hardly ours. Our mixed society, corrupt
though it is, bears little relation to his. Our Church, too, in
numbers and influence, is strong. We in Britain today may
well feel obliged to be as much as possible ' *in* the world ',
with positive Christian purpose, to make saving Christian
impact. But John's verses convey, at least, one timeless
truth: compromise with worldliness means being ' *of* the
world ' as well as *in* it—and if ' of the *world* ' then not ' of
the *Father* '.

So much is still at stake.

15. love of the Father
Better, ' love for the Father ' (RSV).

16. The lust of the eyes
' The tendency to be captivated by the outward show of
things, without enquiring into their real values ' (Dodd).

The pride of life
Hē alazoneia tou biou. Bios, as usually (cp. 3.17; Luke
8.14; 15.12), of life in its external aspect. (Contrast *zōē*).
THE PRIDE (' proud glory ': Moffatt) OF LIFE is pride in one's
worldly possessions: the boastful arrogance of the braggart
(*alazōn*).

not of the Father . . . but of the world
OF, *ek*, here denotes source, origin. Cp. 2.19, 29; 3.8 f., etc.
See note on 3.8. These desires ' have their origin ' not in God

but 'in the finite order in so far as it has become estranged
from God' (Brooke).

LIGHT IMPLIES TRUTH

2.18-28

The concept 'God is light', we have seen, stands for
God's moral perfection (1.5–2.2) and God's self-revelation
as love (2.3-17). In 2.18-28, the concept 'God is light'
(which—though remotely—appears to govern this subsec-
tion also) again expresses God's self-revelation: this time
in terms of *truth*.

The Christian proves he is in the light, John now shows,
not only by righteous life and obedient brotherly love, but
by true belief, i.e. by confession of the truth taught by and
embodied in Jesus Christ (cp. vv. 21, 24 f., 27 f.).

Between 'truth' and 'lie' John makes the same clear-cut
distinction as, earlier, between light and darkness, righteousness and sin, love and hate, love of the Father and love of
the world. 'No lie is of (*ek*) the truth' (v. 21). All denial of
the truth (v. 22), or supplementation of it from worldly
sources (v. 27), is a lie. Further, certain courses of action,
such as withdrawal from (the orthodox) fellowship and out-
going (v. 19) into the world, and teaching of heresy (implicit
in v. 27) by these seducers (v. 26), clearly derive from this
lie-possession.

John finds these policies diametrically opposed to
Jesus Christ and the truth he brought. So much so that
the liars (v. 22) who practise them must be antichrists
(v. 18).

18. *The Last Hour: the Antichrists*
'My children, this is the last hour! You were told that
Antichrist was to come, and now many antichrists have

E

appeared; which proves to us that this is indeed the last
hour' (NEB).

It was an old Jewish myth[1] that before the End evil would
make a desperate last stand in the person of a kind of
devil's Messiah: either a man of diabolical power or a
demonic supernatural being. The word ANTICHRIST here
(and in 2.22; 4.3; II John 7) is its first extant use,[2] and only
John in the New Testament uses it. The idea, however, is
found in the 'false Christs' of Mark 13.22, 'the appalling
horror' of Mark 13.14 (Dan. 12.11), the Man of Sin of
II Thess. 2.3, 8, and the Beast of, e.g., Rev. 19.19 ff.

John discerns the signs of the times. Like Peter at Pentecost, he declares: 'This is that . . .'. He rationalises
(demythologises?) the myth and boldly identifies the heretics with the foretold Antichrist. Hence John knows the
date: IT IS THE LAST HOUR, the immediate prelude to the
Consummation of the Age. In a sense, of course, he was
wrong—like the many since who have believed 'the last
hour' in their own lifetime. In a sense he was surely
also *right*—in his recognition of Antichrist.[3] The seducers
(v. 26) were guilty not only of radically false beliefs, devilish
perversions of Christianity. These they were actually propa-
gating as the very acme of Christian truth, as super-
Christianity! Could there be greater wickedness? John is
sure the heretics embody the Ultimate Lie. They must be
antichrists.

John's trenchant term for the false teachers would have
great practical effect on his readers. No longer could they
be complacently tolerant of the Asian heretics: John had
labelled them ANTICHRISTS! And if anything further were

[1] See Brooke, pp. 69 ff., for a full account of pre-Jewish Babylonian
myths of similar significance.

[2] Introduced without explanation in v. 18. The word must have been
well known.

[3] And those, too, who later spotted him in Nero, Hitler, Stalin, etc.,
were right. We may believe that Antichrist—the idea the term enshrines—
finds recurrent but varied embodiment in each generation of 'the last
days'.

needed to ensure the readers' stiff resistance it was the declaration of the traditional corollary of 'Antichrist-come': THIS IS THE LAST HOUR. In effect: 'This is the eleventh hour, and your last great testing. Hold on now at all costs to the truth you have. Swerve not an inch!' Cp. on II John 8.

19. *The Secession*

A valuable verse, alluding to the event which we take to have prompted the letter.[1] Some Asian church members had left the main body. As will presently appear, they did not disavow Christianity; they claimed, rather, to have superior Christian truth (v. 20). They prophesied (4.1) and taught (2.27), expounding the inadequacies of 'ordinary' Christianity and extolling their compound of Christianity and Cerinthian Gnosticism. They appear to have attracted many. They were themselves many—the 'many antichrists' (v. 18).

Verse 19 treats the single fact—THEY WENT OUT FROM US —and one problem it posed for the faithful. 'How could the seceders do it? Weren't they members of our fellowship?' The reply is, virtually, 'Were they members—*ever*? Surely not. If they had really belonged to us they would never have broken fellowship. Yet God's providence is in their seceding: it is his way whereby they all stand revealed in their true colours, as patently NOT OF US.'

19. of us

i.e. belonging to the Christian community true to the traditional Gospel.

but they went out that they might be made manifest . . .

The clause THAT (*hina*) . . . MADE MANIFEST expresses *purpose*, but God's, not the heretics'. (Cp. the Gospels' 'This was done that (*hina*) it might be fulfilled that . . .')

[1] For the occasion of the letter, nature of the heresy, etc., see pp. 27 ff.

In what the seceders did God's provident purpose was being served. He meant them to be revealed in this way.

that they were not all of us

Greek has 'are', not WERE. Better: 'that they (the heretics)—all of them—have no part or lot with us' (cp. RSV).

THE SECEDERS' CANT EXPOSED

2.20b, 22-23a

Within vv. 20-23 (as in 1.6, 8, 10 and 2.4-11) the seceders are exposed: now for their false belief. The polemic—with which we begin—is again found interlocked with positive teaching for the faithful. The false teaching attacked in vv. 22 f. is explicit; in v. 20 it has to be inferred from John's assurance to the faithful (vv. 20b, 21).

(1) *We alone have spiritual knowledge* (v. 20b)

Seceders (to John's members): Come over and be anointed into our mysteries! Join the spiritual *cognoscenti*! Your present so-called knowledge leaves you ignorant and enslaved. That's all most are fit for, but if you aspire to the real emancipating truth, we have it!

John: You lie! Saving knowledge is for *every*[1] Christian. He has all the truth he needs—and quite enough to detect a lie (and stamp it as alien to the truth) when he hears it![2] You talk of 'anointing'. Even the humblest Christian needs no anointing of yours. He already is anointed—and with the Holy Spirit received from God.

[1] Reading, with the much preferable MSS, *pantes* (all men), not *panta* (all things). So RSV, NEB.

[2] This idea might partly explain 'you know the truth *and know that no lie is of the truth*' in v. 21b.

20. Ye have an unction

RSV: 'You have been anointed.' The noun *chrisma* means (*a*) oil, (*b*) ritual anointing with oil, (*c*) solemn anointing, in a figurative sense. In sense (*c*), for example, Jesus is *Christos*. At his baptism God anointed (*echrisen*) him with the Holy Spirit and with power (Acts 10.38). So here (and in v. 27, q.v. for further commentary on *chrisma*) the UNCTION likeliest is the Christian's anointing with the Holy Spirit by God. (Cp. II Cor. 1.21.)

The verb-form *chriō*, 'anoint', was in common Christian use. Not so, it seems, the noun *chrisma*, current in heretical circles.[1] John is here deliberately borrowing the word. When he says to the faithful: 'You' (the pronoun emphatic, as in v. 27), 'you too have an "anointing",' he is alluding to the heretics' vaunted *chrisma*. What follows means: 'yours is of no questionable nature and origin but is of the Holy Spirit and from the Holy One.'

ye know all things

Follow RSV: 'You all know.' See p. 68 n. 1. John does not mean that (as AV implies) his faithful members have nothing to learn but that ALL of them have sufficient truth for salvation. He is countering the heretics' claim that saving knowledge was only for some and only began with the *gnosis* in which they trafficked.

John looks more closely now at this heretical *gnosis*. His readers, who already (v. 21) KNOW THE TRUTH, will recognise its falsity.

(2) *Jesus is not the Christ* (v. 22)

Seceders: Listen to the truth about Jesus whom you call the Christ. Jesus is human, the Christ altogether divine. How

---

[1] Hippolytus tells us, for example, that initiates of the Naassenes, a sect of Gnostics, were 'anointed at the third portal with speechless *chrisma*'.

naïve you are still to believe them permanently identified!
Was the Christ born? Did the divine suffer and die?
Granted, the Christ came upon Jesus at his baptism and
remained to work the miracles of the ministry; but Jesus
alone was born, Jesus alone suffered and died. These defiling
indignities could never befall the Christ. Before the passion
of Jesus, the Christ sped away back to the divine and spiritual
sphere. To say otherwise borders on blasphemy.

John: You—with your 'truth'—are the blasphemers! For this
is the very heart of Christian truth, that Jesus of Nazareth,
the boy who was born and the man who ministered, suffered,
died, and rose again, was at the same time—and all the time
—the divine Christ, the eternal Son of God the Father. You
who deny this truth—denying both the Father and the Son—
are liars incomparable! Antichrists you are!

(3) *We need no Son to have the Father* (vv. 22b-23)

Seceders: Come now! We are not denying the *Father*; him we
own.

John: Your claim is false. You can't disown Jesus Christ the
(Incarnate) Son and yet own God the Father. Jesus' own
teaching (e.g. Matt. 11.27; 10.32 f.; Mark 8.38) is explicit.
And precisely because he is the Christ, the Son, and because
we know and have *him*, we have the Father too. (Cp. John
1.18; 12.44 f.; 14.9.) You who are without him are also
bound to be without the Father.

22. denieth that Jesus is the Christ

See above for our interpretation—that this is a *Gentile*
Christian heresy. Why not *Jewish* Christian (i.e., a denial
that the Messiah had come)? See pp. 31 f. for discussion.
If we are wrong, THAT JESUS IS THE CHRIST must be used
with *double entendre*, to mean one thing to Jewish, another
to Gentile, heretical Christians. Indubitably the latter are
under fire.

denieth the Father and the Son

Strictly, denial of the Father-Son relationship of Jesus.

Christological error is still the issue. But false views of Jesus Christ mean also false views of *God*. To deny the Son's Sonship is, *ipso facto*, to be in no position to know God: it is TO DENY THE FATHER. (Ritschl is in John's steps in saying: 'Without Christ I should be an atheist.')

23. denieth . . . acknowledgeth

Strong reminiscence here of Matt. 10.32 f., suggests that John is 'basing himself upon the common tradition of early Christianity, incorporating the teaching of Jesus Himself' (Dodd).

he that acknowledgeth the Son hath the Father also

'The confession of Christ establishes solidarity with Him, by which our standing before God is guaranteed' (*ibid.*).

After this wave of attack upon them (vv. 20-23), the heretics stand exposed as no minor deviationists. Their false beliefs (concerning *gnosis* and concerning Jesus Christ) are radical. They are liars and antichrists. Despite their grandiose claims to superior knowledge, they clearly have no standing before God at all!

As John intended (v. 26), his readers would now be open-eyed to the seceders' pernicious 'truth' and to the peril of seduction. More than that, they would be strengthened by John's reminders (within these polemical verses and, later, in vv. 24, 25, 27) of the greatness of their own position. We consider these now.

20-21, 23b-25, 27. *The Blessings of the Light*

John reminds them they already possess the truth (v. 21). They *all* have knowledge (v. 20), for their ordinary church membership entails their receipt from God of the Holy Spirit (v. 20, *chrisma*) whose function it is to teach of all things (v. 27) and whose nature it is to be true (v. 27). From

their first Christian teaching (v. 24) they have known the
saving truth that Jesus is the Christ (v. 22), the divine Son
of God (v. 23). Remaining true to this fundamental doctrine
(v. 24a), they will assuredly continue in communion with
both Son and Father (vv. 23 f.), and thus gain their
promised eternal life (v. 25).

Powerful positive reasons for resisting, from strength, the
seducing would-be teachers (vv. 26 f.)! The truth of Christ
the faithful have is their ample armament against Antichrist.

24. abide in . . . remain in . . . continue in
The same Greek verb, *menein*, for all three English ones.
To CONTINUE IN THE SON in John (e.g. John 15.5 ff.; 6.56) is
'to be "a man in Christ"' in Paul. Both express the believer's intimate communion with Christ.

which ye have heard from the beginning
Their sound Christian doctrine received as catechu-
mens.

27. But the anointing which ye have received of him
YE is emphatically placed, as in v. 20; OF HIM is 'of
Christ', although the parallel 'from the Holy One' (v. 20)
more probably means 'from God'; ABIDE IN HIM (vv. 27 f.)
means 'abide in Christ'.

The ANOINTING (*chrisma*) of the faithful we take to be the
gift of the Holy Spirit. (Cp. v. 20.) Dodd disagrees. He argues
at length that since the heretical *chrisma* is a *gnosis*, a kind
of knowledge, the orthodox *chrisma* meant must also be a
body of teaching, viz. the Gospel, as an indwelling, living,
continually teaching power. But (*a*) the association of the
word *chriein* (if not *chrisma*) is demonstrably not with the
Gospel but with the gift of the Holy Spirit (see on v. 20);
and (*b*) the strong connection of *chrisma* here with teaching

ascribes to the *chrisma* the precise function of the promised Holy Spirit in John 14.26; 16.13.

ye shall abide in him
Present imperative in Greek: 'Continue to abide in him!', i.e. Christ.

26-28. *Don't yield to lies, abide in Christ: his coming will not shame you.*

These verses round off the sub-section 2.18-28. The Elder has written THESE THINGS (v. 26), i.e. vv. 18-25, in warning against the heretics' seductive lies. Now in v. 27 he puts the onus for their continued safety squarely on his flock's own shoulders. His YE NEED NOT THAT ANY MAN TEACH YOU alludes, no doubt, to the heretics' eagerness to impart their pseudo-knowledge. But it is also John's disclaimer of any need—himself—to 'teach' the flock. They all have their *chrisma*, all the knowledge they need for coping with their present crisis: let them use it! Yet John cannot forbear to remind them: ABIDE IN CHRIST! (v. 27).

This fundamental command, introduced by the Elder's intimate pastoral address, LITTLE CHILDREN, is repeated in v. 28 with a final spur to obedience. He means: 'Do not cease to abide in Christ, for remember what time it is (cp. v. 18)! Christ is on his way. Stay true to him now so that you may experience no shrinking shame but a glad fearlessness when the royal visitor arrives.'

28. we may have confidence
See 3.21; 4.17; 5.14, for the other uses in this letter of *parrhēsia*, here translated CONFIDENCE. Etymologically it means 'freedom of speech'. In New Testament usage it conveys the distinctively joyous abandon and fear-free condition of those who live in the light of the Gospel. It is the new-found 'boldness', in face of powerful adversaries, observed in Peter and John in Acts 4.13; the normally

proper 'unreserved confidence' of the Christian's approach to God in prayer and worship (e.g. in I John 3.21 ff.; 5.14 ff.; Heb. 4.16; 10.19); and notably the 'glad fearlessness' which, in this verse and again in 4.17, the Christian is privileged to exhibit before Christ in the day of judgment.

A great New Testament word for one of the great realities of the new age! Perhaps, indeed, *parrhēsia* is itself the greatest of the 'blessings of the light'; its possession implies possession of all else.

at his coming

The word *parousia*, meaning initially presence or advent (as the first stage in presence), acquired a twofold technical sense in the pagan world: (*a*) of 'the coming of a hidden divinity, who makes his presence felt by a revelation of his power', and (*b*) the visit of a king or emperor to a province.[1] From (*b*) particularly comes the Christian technical use of the term, meaning Christ's Messianic advent in glory to judge the world at the end, and to reward the faithful with eternal life.

With v. 28 John reaches the end of the section 2.15-28 and of the first main division of his letter, 1.5–2.28: 'God is light'.

LIFE

2.29–4.6

For symmetry's sake 'God is life' would be a tempting title for this second main division of the letter—between 'God is light' (for the first division) and 'God is love' (for the third). But it would be a little less than justified. Right enough, in 2.29–4.6 we may suspect the thought 'God is

[1] Bauer, *A Lexicon of New Testament Greek*, tr. Arndt and Gingrich, *parousia*, pp. 635-636.

life' at the back of John's mind. And I John 5.11, 20 and
John 1.4; 5.26; 11.25; 14.6 (especially 5.26) do suggest that
'God is life' would be no strange or repugnant idea to him.
But the fact remains that no Scripture ever actually says
outright: 'God is life'. At most, then, we can safely call
the controlling motif of 2.29–4.6 'Life' (meaning 'Eternal
Life') or 'Life in the Family of God' (Dodd).

The phrases IS BORN OF HIM (2.29) and NOW ARE WE THE
CHILDREN OF GOD (RSV, 3.2) at its beginning, WE HAVE
PASSED FROM DEATH UNTO LIFE (3.14) in the middle, and WE
ARE OF (*ek*) GOD (4.6) at its end, span the whole division.
They bind it together, for they are virtually synonymous
terms to describe Christians' distinctive condition. The
middle term, 'life' (3.14), yields our title.

Since Christ the life (John 1.4; 11.25; 14.6) came, those
who 'have (i.e. believe in) the Son have life' (I John 5.11-
12). They live already in the promised new order not only
of 'the true light' but of eternal life (manifested in the
Son) here and now. The old order—the order of death, the
'natural' sphere of fallen, unregenerate man—still lingers
on but it is itself now dying.

When a man becomes a Christian (or 'child of God' or
'born of him') he passes from the one order to the other:
he has 'passed from death unto life' (3.14; cp. John 5.24),
and condemnation and death have no more dominion over
him.

But how can he be sure of having made this 'passage'?
(Or of being a 'child of God'?) By applying the tests of
'life'. To drive home these tests—to show that 'eternal
life' (or 'being a child of God') carries exacting ethical
obligations—is a major concern of the whole letter, and
notably of this division, 2.29–4.6. The sub-divisions make
this plain: Life implies Righteousness (2.29-3.10), Love
(3.11–3.19a), Truth (3.19–4.6). John insists that talk of being
regenerate ('of God', 'children of God', 'born of God',
'passed from death unto life') is no more than talk unless a

man passes these tests: Do you do right (2.29; 3.7)? Do you love your brother (3.14)? Do you act truly (3.18-19) and believe what is true (3.23; 4.2)?

LIFE IMPLIES RIGHTEOUSNESS

2.29–**3.**10

29. *Right-doing proves you born of God*

The verse strictly says: 'As you know Christ is righteous, you may be sure every man who does right is Christian'[1]— *not*, as logic expects, 'you may be sure the Christian does right' (Cp. 3.3, 5 f.). What is John's point here? Is he really making unconscious Christians out of, say, conscientious right-doing humanists? A most un-Johannine idea! John surely has in mind only professing Christians, and means: 'You may be sure that every professing Christian who does right is a Christian in deed and truth.'

if ye know that he is righteous . . .

The idea (and movement into this new main division) comes from thought of Christ's righteousness to be reckoned with at his *parousia*, v. 28.

he is righteous . . . born of him

Who is HE? God or Christ? In v. 28 IN HIM, BEFORE HIM, HIS COMING, all refer to Christ. So must also HE IS RIGHTEOUS, coming in the very next clause (v. 29a). The only difficulty is in BORN OF HIM. In the same sentence HE and OF HIM ought to stand for the same person, i.e. '*Christ* is righteous' should mean that BORN OF HIM is 'born of *Christ*'. But whereas 'born of God' is a favourite Johannism (cp. 3.9; 4.7; 5.1, 4, 18), John never—with

---

[1] 'Born of him' (like 'child of God', 'passed unto life') is tantamount to 'Christian'.

certainty—writes 'born of Christ'. Here, too, BORN OF HIM
is most probably 'born of *God*' even although HE IS
RIGHTEOUS is '*Christ* is righteous'. Strict grammar is vio-
lated, as not uncommonly in I John.

2.29–3.1. *Born of him . . . children of God*

The word 'regenerate'—or 'Christian'—conveys most of
the significance of both phrases. But we must look a little
more closely at their rationale.[1] They are terms of great
importance in this letter.

Natural birth (mediated by human parents) relates us all
as creatures to the life-giving Creator. But there is another
birth, entirely of God's gift and initiative. Those who accept
it are BORN OF HIM. They become no longer merely creatures
of their Creator but CHILDREN OF GOD their Father. (This
change is the transition [3.14] from the order of death to
that of life.) They become 'like him'.[2] (Cp. also the Fourth
Gospel references, 1.12 f.; 3.1-8, to 'becoming children of
God' and 'being born again'.) With him they form the
family of God. In the Christian era this family is the Church
fellowship.

We recall generally similar teaching in both the Synoptics and Paul. The Synoptic 'being in the kingdom' and the
Pauline 'being in Christ' are (like John's 'being born of
God') not natural states but states of grace into which God
has called some, and in which they are (adopted) sons
(*huioi*) and he is Father.

But John's terminology—'birth from God', 'children
(*tekna*, not *huioi*) of God'—is different. How significant is
the difference?

We suspect, with Dodd, that the phrase BORN OF GOD is
here deliberately used because 'like "knowing God" and
"being in the light"' it 'was an expression used, and in our

---

[1] Full discussion is beyond our space. See Dodd, pp. 65-68, to which
our own note is indebted.

[2] Cp. I John 3.2 and notes.

author's view misused, by the false teachers '.[1] Divine regeneration through *gnosis*-initiation is a feature of Hellenistic mysticism. ' The antecedents of the idea of regeneration '
(unlike that of sonship by adoption) ' lie not within Judaism,
but in Hellenistic thought.'[2]

Yet John himself is not to be thought to have ' gone
Greek ' *in his own use* of these terms of Hellenism. For one
thing, as Dodd allows, Matt. 5.9 ' they shall be called the
sons (*huioi*) of God ' (cp. Matt. 5.45) lies behind John's ' that
we should be called the children (*tekna*) of God ' (I John 3.1).
He further comments (p. 69): ' In Johannine circles it
appears that the term " Son of God " was reserved exclusively for the " only-begotten Son " and the term " children "
(*tekna* not *huioi*) substituted when believers were spoken
of.' In John's own mind, then, *tekna theou* may simply be
the Synoptic *huioi theou* reverentially altered. For himself,
the associations of ' children of God ' will be Jewish and
Christian, not Hellenistic.

More certain is the actual manner in which John treats
the theme of ' birth from God ' in the letter. He is adamant
about its ethical connotation. His aim all the time is to
show that, in this, what *he* means by CHILDREN OF GOD
differs *toto caelo* from what the Hellenistic mystery-mongers
and the heretics mean.

3.1. Behold what manner of love

The chapter opens on a note of wonder. Moffatt catches
it when he takes up the phrase BORN OF HIM (2.29), gratui-
tously repeats it thus, ' " Born of Him! " ', and continues :
' Think what a love the Father has for us . . . ! ' So also
the beautiful opening of the Scottish Paraphrase :

> Behold the amazing gift of love
> The Father hath bestowed
> On us, the sinful sons of men
> To call us sons of God !

[1] Dodd, p. 68.   [2] *Ibid.*

Both versions do justice to *potapos*, WHAT MANNER OF
(AV). The word suggests surprise mingled with admiration.
Cp. Mark 13.1.

1-2. *You are God's children*

(1) *In name and fact, now.* The greatness of God's love
lies in his letting us, such as we are, be called his children
(cp. Matt. 5.9); implicitly, too, in his letting us call him
' Abba, Father '.

But the name is only the first of wonders. John adds—
still v. 1—a phrase AV omits: ' And so we are ' (RSV). The
Greek, *kai esmen*, terse and forceful, cries: ' This is no
mere name: this is *fact*! We *are* children of God! '

To make sense of the second half of v. 1, imagine an
objector (a disheartened Christian reader) countering ' And
so we are ' with ' But the world sees nothing special about
" God's children ".' THEREFORE, answers John, THE WORLD
KNOWETH US NOT, BECAUSE IT KNEW HIM NOT. In other
words: ' Why be surprised? Pagan society refused to recognise God in creation or history. Above all, it failed to discern the divine Son of God in the man Jesus. What hope,
then, for recognition of the SONS (*tekna*, strictly ' children ')
OF GOD? '

The first verse's total impact on the dispirited would be:
' Be not dismayed! Expect the world's blindness! You bear
a great name standing for a tremendous reality; accomplished   present fact. By God's amazing grace you are
—in spite of appearances—God's children, at this very
moment.'

(2) *With a greater future still.* Verse 2 picks up the ' And
so we are ' (v. 1, RSV) and repeats it with the emphatic NOW.
NOW ARE WE THE SONS OF GOD. This NOW serves a double
purpose. It underlines the Christian's present greatness as
child of God compared with his past state of mere natural
birth. It also introduces the contrast between the Christian's
present NOW, great as it is, with his yet more glorious future.

This is the climax of the wonder with which the chapter-opening is instinct. The glory of our earthly state of sonship does not exhaust God's plan for us. Ahead of what WE ARE is WHAT WE SHALL BE. Whatever this future will involve —and IT DOTH NOT YET APPEAR—what is yet to be is better than even our earthly best. For, amid so much unknown in that future, this much *is* known and sure: that WHEN HE SHALL APPEAR WE SHALL BE LIKE HIM, FOR WE SHALL SEE HIM AS HE IS. The believer's final assured goal is seeing God[1] AS HE IS, beholding 'without a veil, his face'. Cp. I Cor. 13.12; Col. 3.4; Matt. 5.8. And this 'seeing' will produce in us, in perfect degree, that conformity to his likeness (cp. Rom. 8.29) in character which, in germ, marks the true child of God on earth, and which we must here and now nurture to the utmost (v. 3).

This then is our assured, magnificent future hope: we shall be with Christ (John 14.3) in the Father's house: WE SHALL SEE HIM: WE SHALL BE LIKE HIM.

(3) *Incognito till he comes.* Much is hidden from us, and about us, in our earthly experience. The world does not recognise children of God when it sees them. In a measure, Christ, even to us, is 'incognito', his glory veiled from mortal sight. And to ourselves today, our future selves— in the fulness of what our 'being like him' means—are 'incognito'. But WHEN HE SHALL APPEAR, then is the moment of manifested truth.

We whose LIFE (whose God-born, God-like nature) is 'hid with Christ in God' (Col. 3.3) shall be revealed to the world as the children of God (cp. Rom. 8.19); the glorious Christ (and God) will be seen AS HE IS; and we shall enter upon the realisation of what we are to be, perfect in Divine fellowship and Christlikeness.

---

[1] 'Him' may stand for Christ, not God, in its second as well as its first usage in v. 2. *N'importe!* For John, to see Christ is to see the Father (John 14.9).

3. *To see him then be like him now*

After two verses which scale the heights, John charac-
teristically brings his readers right down to earth. EVERY
MAN THAT HATH THIS HOPE (i.e. of seeing God or Christ then,
as he is, and of being like him then) IN HIM (i.e. in Christ,
based upon Christ) PURIFIETH HIMSELF, EVEN AS HE (*ekeinos*,
John's usual word for Christ) IS PURE.

This hope ahead is an *assured* hope. The Greek, 'have
hope', is considerably stronger than 'hope' *simpliciter*
would be. It is no licence to moral laxity, but rather the
strongest of incentives to Christlike purity *now*. To John
this is inescapable logic for all who, 'born of God', qualify
for THIS HOPE. John will allow no special cases, such as the
Gnostic heretics ('hope'-ful yet morally indifferent) may
have claimed to be. By EVERY MAN John tilts already, as
he will more clearly in vv. 4-9, at these would-be exceptions.

purifieth himself

Hagnizei: the verb used of the high-priest's self-
purification before entering the Holy of Holies. Its appositeness here is evident. But no mere ritual purity—which might
have satisfied Gnostic or Jewish requirements—is in John's
mind. Rather is it that personal moral purity of heart without which no man shall see God (Matt. 5.8).

even as he is pure

i.e., after the pattern of Christ's own absolute purity
which fits him for the Father's presence. (For the tense, see
on v. 7, EVEN AS HE IS RIGHTEOUS.)

THE SECEDERS' CANT EXPOSED

3.4-9

In vv. 4-9 three phrases suggest that John has Gnostics in
general, the seceding heretics in particular, in mind. They

F

are: v. 4, WHOSOEVER (Greek, every man who) COMMITTETH
SIN TRANSGRESSETH THE LAW; v. 7, HE THAT DOETH RIGHT-
EOUSNESS IS RIGHTEOUS . . .; v. 9, WHOSOEVER IS BORN OF
(Greek, every man born of) GOD DOTH NOT COMMIT SIN . . .
V. 4 conceals the claim of some to superiority over moral
law; v. 6, to possession of a peculiar 'righteousness' indif-
ferent to right-doing; v. 9, to 'birth from God' with no
obligation to shun sin.

How does John expose and answer them? As in 1.6, 8,
10; 2.4-11; 2.22-23a, we attempt to bring out the implicit
dialogue.

(1) 'We are above the moral law' (vv. 4-6)

Seceders: You say you are God's children. We say *we* are. Our
divine regeneration means that we are *super*-human: bound
no longer by any, even the moral, law. There are 'lesser
breeds *within* the law', but we are above it, as we are above
them. We are free to act as we please. Even if we 'sin' (as
you put it), we break no law that affects us.

John: But the law is valid for you still. It is the very law of
man's being, every man's. Like every one else's, your sin is
sin and—therefore—breaks that valid law (v. 4). Further, by
your sins (and indifference to them) you are 'stultifying the
whole purpose of the Incarnation'[1] which was TO TAKE
AWAY . . . SINS (v. 5). Above all: in view of your sins
and attitude to sin, how can you be 'God-born' when IN
HIM IS NO SIN (v. 5b)? Where's your kinship? Why, your
persistent sinning means your separation from God (or
Christ), your ignorance of him and blindness to him (v. 6)!

4. Sin is the transgression of the law

'Sin is lawlessness' (RSV). The *anomia* here is not wild
Gnostic antinomianism. John means 'failures to fulfil the
law of love, rather than grosser sins of the flesh . . . hardly,
perhaps never, referred to in this Epistle' (Brooke). The

[1] Brooke, p. 85.

point made is: all sin—sin in its essence—is defiance of
God's revealed will.

5. to take away our sins

Obvious allusion to John 1.29, 'taketh away the sin of
the world'. (Note: 'sin' in the Gospel, SINS here, as in
I John 1.9; 2.2. Typically, I John makes the Gospel truth
more concrete.) To sin is a grave matter, for 'sin undoes
the work of Christ. . . . It is to bring back and to multiply
that sin which He came into the world to destroy.'[1]

in him is no sin

Cp. John 7.18; II Cor. 5.21; Heb. 4.15.

6. Whosoever abideth in him sinneth not

Apparently flat contradiction of 1.8-10—and of experience. A partial explanation may be in the present tense here
used. The Greek present denotes habitual, persistent action.
Hamartanei is 'keeps on sinning'. (So also the tenses in
3.9, 'doth not commit', 'cannot', sin.) John means, then:
'When a man abides in Christ it is not his normal practice
to sin.' This truth follows naturally enough upon IN HIM IS
NO SIN. If Christ is sinless no Christian can have sin as his
settled policy.

Yet does this completely explain the crux? Would John
have trusted so much to readers' grasp of a grammatical
subtlety? Unlikely. Besides, the puzzling fact remains that
in 1.8 the heretics are dubbed self-deceivers for saying 'we
have no sin' (also present tense, with habitual, persistent
force), which very thing John seems to affirm here (3.6) to
be Christian truth.

The key is that 1.8 and 3.6 address different heretical conditions. (See on 1.8; pp. 49 f.) The former tells the *com-
placent,* convinced of their moral perfection: 'You are
deceiving yourselves.' The latter tells the morally *indifferent,*

[1] Barclay, *The Letters of John,* p. 89.

convinced that their super-humanity as 'children of God' placed them above the moral law: 'No Christian makes a steady habit of sin.'[1]

Grammar and context in conjunction unlock most, if not all, of the verse's perplexities. So also in v. 9.

(2) 'We have a special righteousness' (v. 7)

Seceders: Don't you realise that we are rendered 'righteous' through our mystic rites and spiritual rebirth? They make us 'right with God' and that's the only righteousness that counts. Actions are irrelevant.

John: Nonsense—and deceitful nonsense at that! Whatever more subtle and profound is true about 'righteousness',[2] this is as plain as a pikestaff: the righteous man does righteous things, after the pattern of Jesus Christ the righteous.

7. Little children

The warmly affectionate pastoral note adds force to John's earnest warning: LET NO MAN DECEIVE YOU. His readers were deception-prone, we gather, and Gnostic deceit was in the air. They must not be 'bamboozled' by any sophistry, however plausible, however prominent its source (this is perhaps the force of NO MAN), 'which blurs the plain meaning' (Dodd) of sin and righteousness. Righteousness is doing right: sin is doing wrong.

even as he is righteous

Righteousness is known by its fruits and its exemplar is Christ.

Note that in the three analogous expressions EVEN AS HE IS PURE (v. 3), AND IN HIM IS NO SIN (v. 5), and, here, EVEN AS HE IS RIGHTEOUS, the present tense is used. A past tense,

---

[1] The 3.6 situation is thus, on closer inspection, that of 1.6, not 1.8.
[2] E.g. the Pauline doctrine of righteousness (or justification) by faith.

referring to the *incarnate* purity, sinlessness and righteousness of Christ might seem more natural. Doubtless the
earthly phase of Christ's life was most in John's mind, but
in all three cases ' the statement is made of the whole human
life of the Christ, and is not confined to the earthly part of
it ' (Brooke). Cp. 4.17; contrast 2.6, ' as he walked '.

(3) *'We are born of God'* (vv. 8-9).

Seceders: Through initiation into our mysteries we are not
   what we used to be.[1] Born of God, we are become other
   persons.[2] We have new and God-like natures.
John: How can you possibly assert this and still sin and be
   indifferent to sin? Far from being ' born of God ', the regular
   sinner belongs to the devil. (To whom else? The devil has
   been sinning from the very first.) Now, what was the purpose
   of the coming of the Son of God? It was to *destroy* the
   works of the devil (for that's what men's sins are)! (v. 8).
   Nobody, then, ' born of God ' makes a habit of sin. After
   all, God's children,[3] like his Son, abide in him. A man's
   ' birth from God ' makes it morally impossible for him to
   be an habitual sinner (v. 9).

8. is of (*ek*) the devil

See on 2.16, 19 and the extended footnote in Dodd, p. 66
(on 2.29–3.10), or Barclay, pp. 106-107 (on 4.1-7), for the
meaning of *ek* (of) in these contexts. Moffatt translates by
' belongs to '. This meets most cases adequately. The root
idea in *ek* is of point of origin. Cp. Heb. 2.11, *ex henos*:
' are of one stock ': ' have all one origin ' (RSV). Sometimes
the idea is weakened, in context, to vague indication of
dependent relation; sometimes strengthened, as in 3.10, *ek
tou theou*, and in 3.8 *ek tou diabolou*, to mean exactly
gegennēmenos ek ' born of '—e.g. in ' born of God ' (v. 9).

[1] *Corp. Hermet.* XIII 2.3.
[2] Hermetic Tract on Regeneration.
[3] See discussion on ' his seed ' (v. 9) below.

the devil sinneth from the beginning

The beginning (*a*) of his existence or (*b*) of sinning, i.e. before the Fall of Adam, Gen. 3. The translation is best kept as vague as the Greek: viz. 'from the first'. Cp. John 8.44. Barclay[1] takes *ap' archēs* logically, not temporally, and interprets: 'The devil sins as a matter of principle.' Even if not the likeliest translation of *ap' archēs*, this makes fair comment on the devil, and John's meaning here. At no time has the devil not sinned: *c'est son raison d'être*.

the works of the devil

The devil has caused Adam's sin and all human sin since. THE WORKS OF THE DEVIL are thus men's sins. To DESTROY (Greek, 'undo') these Christ came. Cp. 3.5.

9. his seed remaineth in him

Lit. 'a seed of him remaineth in him.' The crux here is the meaning of SEED, *sperma*. (1) Dodd takes SEED as the divine principle immanent in man.[2] For John, says Dodd, this meant the word of God (i.e. the Gospel), which so regenerates men that they do not sin. James 1.18 and I Peter 1.23-25 support this. (2) Moffatt interprets SEED as 'offspring'; HIS SEED, as a synonym for 'whosoever is born of God'. For *sperma* in sense of 'offspring' cp. Luke 1.55; Gal. 3.29; John 8.33, 37. The thought (on this interpretation) is precisely that of 3.6: 'whosoever abideth in him sinneth not.'

The alternatives thus are (N.B. the pronouns): (1) for a seed of Him (i.e. a seed of God; RSV, 'God's nature') abides in him (the believer), or (2) for His seed (i.e. God's offspring) abides in Him (God).

Evidence is very evenly balanced between them. NEB follows Dodd. We prefer Moffatt's simpler view. The fact

[1] *Op. cit.*, p. 90.
[2] The heretic Valentinus spoke of the divine seed which resides in good souls.

that it makes John tautologous need not tell against its probability!

he cannot sin (*harmartanein*, present tense), **because he is born of God**

The strongest of the series of perplexing statements (vv. 6-9) on the 'sinlessness' of the Christian. See the commentary on v. 6 as it bears on v. 9.

Two points must be held together. (*a*) John knows perfectly well that the Christian *can* sin: he has lapses. See 1.8; 2.1, etc. (*b*) John is asserting here that the Christian cannot, without creating an impossible moral contradiction, deliberately and consistently sin. (Born of God who is good, how can he set himself to sin which is of the devil?)

On the issue for interpretation which these statements in vv. 6-9 present, Brooke's remark (p. 90) merits heed: 'The writer speaks . . . here . . . in the absolute language of the prophet rather than with the circumspection of the casuist.'

4-9. *Rebirth outlaws sin in you*

In vv. 4-9 this prophetic voice has been raised, as we have seen, against the heretics. The immediate audience, nevertheless, has been the faithful flock. This passage has been full of warning and heart-searching of the most challenging kind to orthodox believers. 'Don't be deceived', John calls to them. Nothing of this heretical infection must invade their soundness. They are to see sin clearly for what it is, as belonging to the devil and so without place in God's child. Birth from God outlaws sin in them. Possession of 'life' intrinsically implies righteousness, and what is righteousness but doing right?

The author's argument is crudely black-and-white. If it repels us today, and if we long for grey, it may betoken our healthy anxiety to state spiritual truth with nicety; it may betoken our own habitual resting in the grey, in belief and conduct. For John that grey is black. Is he wrong?

10. *The children's deeds reveal their father*

'By this test (*en toutō*) the children of God and the children of the devil are plainly distinguished' (v. 10a). By what test? That of v. 10b: WHOSOEVER DOETH NOT RIGHT-EOUSNESS IS NOT OF GOD, NEITHER HE THAT LOVETH NOT HIS BROTHER. Such men brand themselves the devil's children. The practice of righteousness and love, we are left to understand, stamps the children of God, equally clearly, with 'whose they are'.

This verse acts as a kind of summary of the argument which began at 2.29. Its clause, however, NEITHER HE THAT LOVETH NOT HIS BROTHER, reinforcing HE THAT DOETH NOT RIGHTEOUSNESS, reintroduces the word LOVE (absent since 2.3-17) into the argument. It leads smoothly into the next section of the second 'cycle':

LIFE IMPLIES LOVE

3.11-19a

John has written pungently in 2.29-3.10 (Life implies Righteousness) about Christian and non-Christian in relation to sin and righteousness, the devil and God. Now, as pungently, he relates Christian and non-Christian to love and hate and their correlatives, life and death. This is John's favourite theme and the terminology of this section he has made, among New Testament writers, specially his own.

The two sections are closely linked. For John the law is summed up in Christ's command to love. Unrighteousness, sin, law-breaking (v. 4) are, therefore, for him, equivalents or synonyms for *failure to love*. 'Sin is lovelessness: love is right-doing' would express this profound Johannine conviction which binds together 2.29–3.10 and 3.11-19a.

11. *Brotherly love your original 'must'*

For this is the message that ye heard from the beginning, that we should love one another

This is why the non-lover of the brethren (v. 10b) is marked out as no child of God, but of the devil, because (FOR) God's message through Christ was, from the first, 'Love one another'.

from the beginning

The last of eight usages of this phrase in I John. (It reappears in II John 5 f.) THE BEGINNING is that of the readers' Christian experience, the commandment—called MESSAGE here—being part of the original Gospel. Cp. 2.7.

one another

Cp. 'brother' (v. 10); 'brethren' (v. 14). Do not take John to *restrict* the Christian's love to his brethren in Christian fellowship. The writer of, say, John 3.16 and I John 2.2, could not but recognise the Christian's obligation to universal love, such as Christ taught in the Sermon on the Mount and exemplified in his life and death.

Yet the stress on love of 'brethren' and 'one another' in the membership of the Christian society has good reason behind it.

(1) In this form and context Christ gave the commandment (John 15.12).[1]

(2) The false teachers—who claimed to be Christians—were signally failing to love their fellow-Christians.

(3) 'The experience of a lifetime . . . would seem to have taught the writer the necessity of charity *beginning* at home.'[2] Paul felt the need too. 'Let us do good unto all men, especially unto them who are of the household of faith' (Gal. 6.10).

[1] In John's Gospel tradition, that is.
[2] Brooke, p. 91.

12-15. *The marks of Cain, the devil's child*

These verses are rather tangled. All is well, however, if we hold fast their main thread: the contrast between Christian and non-Christian expressed, as sharply and forcefully as possible, in terms of love and hate, life and death, righteousness and evil. Verse 13 is just an aside, in parenthesis, evoked by v. 12.

To point his contrast John exploits the Old Testament story of Cain.[1] He makes Cain his type of the non-Christian, and calls him the devil's child (v. 12). He is characterised by hate, murder, exclusion from eternal life.

John, we consider, has the instance of Cain still in mind when framing vv. 14b-15. To produce their general statements HE THAT LOVETH NOT HIS BROTHER ABIDETH IN DEATH . . . WHOSOEVER HATETH HIS BROTHER IS A MURDERER . . . NO MURDERER HATH ETERNAL LIFE ABIDING IN HIM, he universalises what was literally true in the actual case of Cain—of an actual brother and a literal murder.

They gravely warn anyone who doubts the seriousness of not loving the brethren. 'If you do not love you hate, and if you hate you murder, and your hate and murder show you to belong, like Cain, to the devil and the domain of death.'

12. And wherefore slew he him?

John's answer is hardly justified by the spare and puzzling account in Gen. 4.1-16. But his guess—that the righteous Abel's murder was assured by the generally evil character of Cain, bound to issue in evil deeds—is no less satisfactory than those of Philo and the writer of Hebrews (Heb. 11.4). John's principle, at any rate, is sound. Violent deeds, and murder their climax, express 'that antipathy which righteousness always' evokes in 'those who make evil their life's guiding principle'.[2]

[1] John's one and only explicit Old Testament reference in the Epistles.
[2] Brooke, p. 92.

Was it not a major factor in the death of Jesus at the hands of evil men that they were galled unbearably by his perfect goodness?

13. Marvel not, my brethren, if the world hate you

Prompted by v. 12. The conflict of Cain and Abel explains why hatred from the evil world is to be expected by Christians walking in righteousness.

14. *Brotherly love the Christian birthmark*

Much less is said within vv. 12-15 on the Christian side of the contrast, but that less—v. 14—is weighty enough to be ample.[1] WE KNOW THAT WE HAVE PASSED FROM DEATH UNTO LIFE BECAUSE WE LOVE THE BRETHREN. A singularly beautiful verse. This is the test and guarantee of our having made the great transition from the realm of death to that of life, that brotherly love is present in our hearts.

passed from death unto life . . .

LIFE is the exclusive possession and sphere of the Christian, the new man in the new age now begun. To PASS FROM DEATH UNTO LIFE, as well as being synonymous with becoming a child of God, being of God, or being born of God, is John's equivalent for the Synoptic 'being saved' and 'entering the kingdom'. Analogous also is I Peter 2.9, 'called out of darkness into his (God's) marvellous light'.

because we love

This LIFE, inseparable from love, is proved present in us by the presence of love. Similarily 'the man who does not love' shows thereby that he 'is still in the realm of death' (NEB).

[1] And it is developed and underlined in vv. 16-19a and 4.7-21.

15. Whosoever hateth

A synonym of 'he that loveth not' (v. 14b). Not to love is to hate. Between love and hate, as between life and death, there is no middle position.

is a murderer

What is the basis of this startling statement? Probably John 8.37-47, in which, at 8.44, Jesus calls the devil a murderer; and Matt. 5.21-22 also provides 'authority . . . for treating hatred as constructive murder'.[1] Even so, the most immediate thought-context of the statement is surely the actual instance of 'typical' Cain on which John has just been dwelling.

ye know that no murderer hath eternal life abiding in him

YE KNOW appeals to the readers' own experience and common sense. It is axiomatic that a man of such character as to murder cannot be indwelt by eternal life, for ETERNAL LIFE is a quality of life which mirrors truly the character and purpose of God.

16a. *The Meaning of Love*

Hereby perceive we the love of God, because he laid down his life for us

Omit OF GOD, not in the original text. Read: 'Hereby perceive we "love", because. . . .'

In this great verse John removes all vagueness from his term LOVE. 'By this we know love, that he laid down his life for us' (RSV). The meaning of LOVE (*agapē*) has been defined, once and for all, in the concrete act of Christ in giving his life for us.[2]

It *needed* definition. Not only the idea of Christian love

[1] Dodd, p. 83. Cp. Barclay, p. 96.
[2] See Dodd's brilliant pp. 84-87, 110-112; also, on *agapē*, G. B. Caird, *The Truth of the Gospel*, pp. 112 f.

was new. The very New Testament noun for it, *agapē*, was practically unknown in non-biblical Greek. The verb *agapan* was in common speech but meant merely 'to be content with', 'to esteem', 'to prefer'. It was 'a comparatively cool and colourless word'.[1] Colour was first given to *agapē* in LXX, the Greek Old Testament. Its translators chose it as the distinctive word for God's love to man and man's responsive love to God.

Then Paul (e.g. I Cor. 13), John (e.g. John 3.16 and I John 3.16; 4.7-21) and others baptised the word into Christ. They gave it beauty, intensity and depth of meaning that were all its own. By *agapē* they meant its LXX meaning 'fulfilled', i.e. 'God's love to man as supremely shown in the gift (and life and death) of Christ' and 'man's answering love to God and his brother, in keeping with that divine love in Christ'.

None of this richness (we remember) inhered in the linguistic roots of *agapē*. Pagans must have been mystified by the Christians' honouring of the word. Converts would need to learn its uniquely Christian meaning: established Christians, to be kept in mind of it. John's readers, none too clear, it seems, on many points of faith and practice, and surrounded by pagans and 'advanced' heretical Christians, would, more than most, need to have repeatedly hammered home to them (as is done in this letter) the precise meaning and demand of *agapē*.

'This is love' (says John); 'Christ giving his life for us.' That is, love means self-giving and self-sacrifice, utterly pure and unreserved, on behalf of others.

Thus Christian *agapē* is set quite apart in meaning from the two common Greek words *philia* (friendship) and *erōs* (love). *Philia* is affection between kindred spirits (such as David and Jonathan).[2] *Erōs*[3] is, at its lowest, physical

---

[1] Dodd, p. 111.
[2] James 4.4 is the only instance in the New Testament.
[3] Absent from the New Testament.

desire; at its highest (e.g. in Plato), the upward surge of the human soul to the ideal world of absolute beauty and truth. It is essentially self-centred and grasping, seeking its own satisfaction by acquiring some desired object. N.B. the object of *erōs* is always *desired because conceived to be good* and worth possessing.

Distinctions may be rather over-sharply drawn in the summing-up '*Erōs* is all take; *Philia* is give-and-take; *Agapē* is all give',[1] but it is substantially true.

And first and foremost *agapē* is *God's* 'give', the downward drive of the divine self-giving—and that not of the Son alone, for in the Son's love we see the *Father's* (cp. John 14.9; 13.1-4; 15.13 f.; 10.11-18, 27-30; 3.16 etc.).

This divine love then finds its response in man's love, to God (e.g. I John 3.17) and to the brethren. This also is called *agapē*. Like God's love,[2] and unlike *erōs*, it is spontaneous, self-giving and *indifferent to the merit of the object loved*. So, we may conclude, *agapē* is at once the nature of God, the meaning of Christ's sacrifice and the badge of his disciples.

16b. *Love, thus defined, is your brother's due.*

Christ's love and the Christian's love are now drawn together. Christ has demonstrated love. He did so, *par excellence*, when he showed self-sacrifice, laying down his life on our behalf. AND WE ('we too', *kai hēmeis*, emphatic) OUGHT TO LAY DOWN OUR LIVES FOR THE BRETHREN. Why the OUGHT? Generally, (1) because 'life' in us implies love and Christ has thus defined love, and, again, (2) because such self-sacrificial love must evoke like love in us. More particularly, (3) because this example has been set by Christ for Christians' imitation.

[1] G. B. Caird, *op. cit.* p. 112.

[2] Cp. Rom. 5.8: 'God proves his love toward us in that, while we were yet sinners, Christ died for us'; also cp. Luke 15 (the Prodigal Son) and Matt. 20 (the Labourers in the Vineyard).

Imitatio Christi is explicitly enjoined in the foot-washing narrative, John 13.12-15, which might be in John's mind here.[1]

17-19a. *Fine talk won't suffice. Prove your love, in present action.*

To our author fine phrases are suspect, even his own! The noble statement 'we ought to lay down our lives for the brethren', he is quick to discern, invites cant. Someone, even a loyal member, may say: 'Amen! I await the great occasion and shall steel myself to show my love in that "supreme sacrifice",' and yet, brought face to face today with a brother in poverty, will shut his heart and his full purse tight against his brother's relief. John stings such a man to shame. HOW DWELLETH THE LOVE OF GOD IN HIM? (v. 17.) In short, if our professed love is to be believed at all, we have to act self-sacrificially, *now*,[2] in our utterly every-day circumstances. Cp. James 2.16.

Jesus is the best commentary and example. Having 'stedfastly set his face to go to Jerusalem' (Luke 9.51), he cast out a dumb spirit and healed a blind beggar and a hunch-backed woman long before his journey's end. His gaze upon the Cross did not blind him to Zacchaeus or the ten lepers. The immediate need of all—serious enough yet relatively 'ordinary'—he fully met, 'in', as the Scots say, 'the by-going'.

Without these self-denying acts—these little crosses lining the way to Calvary—could we ever have been quite sure that on Calvary itself Jesus laid down his life for us in love? In our case, we credibly protest our readiness to 'give our all' for our fellows (in that heroic moment which our life-

[1] Like John, Paul and Peter do not fear to speak of 'imitating' Christ. Cp. I Cor. 11.1; I Peter 2.21.

[2] Just how well the spirit of the supreme self-sacrifice on the Cross may be concentrated in ordinary benevolence is seen in the widow's two-mite offering, 'even all her living' (Mark 12.41-44).

time may never present) only if, as we go, we never balk at
the giving of a sacrificial shilling, or hour of time, or service
through our talents, for the relief of John Smith's problem
now.

So, 'let us put our love not into words or into talk but
into deeds, and make it real. Thus it is that we may be sure
we belong to the truth . . .' (vv. 18-19a, Moffatt).

17. this world's good

Bios. ' Goods ', we would say. NEB: ' If a man has enough
to live on . . .'

the love of God
i.e. ' love *for* God.'

19. and hereby we know that we are of the truth
Here OF THE TRUTH means almost ' of God '. Take
HEREBY with a backward reference; i.e., we know we are
OF THE TRUTH by love made real in action (v. 18).

With WE ARE OF THE TRUTH we believe the sentence
should end. With it ends the sub-division: Life implies Love
(3.11-3.19a). Yet the phrase OF THE TRUTH (like ' born of
him ', 2.29) is a kind of swing-door. It leads into the next
sub-division:

LIFE IMPLIES TRUTH

3.19–4.6

This section is most simply regarded as bound together
—albeit very loosely—by the single idea ' Life implies
Truth '.

We attempt to set out the thought-progression below, in
three parts:

3.19-23. *Your truth your assurance before God*

Thought of THE TRUTH in the being, doing, and believing of sincere Christians probably lies behind the beautiful but perplexing vv. 19b-22. Because of this essential TRUTH in them, true Christians in the presence of God—who is himself true (5.20)—are where they belong.

Aware of shortcoming, they may be diffident (v. 20a) about approaching God. They can reassure themselves. God will assess them by a standard more reliable than their feelings (their HEART). He KNOWETH ALL THINGS. If comfort is John's meaning here (see below) then surely it is that, *inter alia*, GOD KNOWETH these Christians' fundamental truth and accord with him—and for their truth's sake accepts. Suppose these sincere Christians come before God untroubled by even initial diffidence. They come confidently (v. 21) and have their petitions granted (v. 22a). On what ground? John states it clearly—their keeping of God's commands (of love and true belief) and their doing of what is pleasing in his sight (vv. 22-23): in short, their ' truth ' (cp. vv. 18-19a, Moffatt).

19-20. A notorious crux. Take the first clause, AND HEREBY WE KNOW THAT WE ARE OF THE TRUTH, as looking back to v. 18b and forming the completion of its sentence. (See p. 96.) Thus it is not involved in the grammatical tangle of vv. 19b-20. We limit ourselves to two alternative interpretations.[1] The Greek—not in itself decisive between them—does yield these two main possible meanings:

(1) *A Warning:* ' But in his presence we shall (do well to) convince our heart that, if even our own heart condemn us, God is greater than our heart and knows everything.'

[1] For a full discussion of the problem of these verses see Dodd, pp. 88-92.

G

(2) *A Comfort:* ' And in his presence we shall reassure our heart, whenever our heart condemn us; because God is greater than our heart and knows everything.'

The first, supported by many Greek Fathers, and in line with the severity of vv. 3-8, 15, 17, means:

' Don't decide too easily that you love in deed and truth and are therefore " of the truth ". Even your own heart tells you that your sincerity in love could, now and then, be questioned. Yet you don't know the half of your failure to make love real in action. God knows it all. What do you think *he* is going to make of you? '

The second means:

' Do not fret despairingly over your imperfections. Be reassured! God knows them, but he who knows all also knows human weakness. He knows your frame and remembers that you are dust. Moreover, he knows that basic soundness and will to be sincere in practical love which is yours, despite your aberrations.'

This comforting interpretation is to be preferred. Grammar apart, the tenor of the context is decisive. ' The aim of the whole passage is surely to give assurance, and not to strike terror into their (the readers') hearts ' (Brooke).

21. if our heart condemn us not

The same people as in v. 20, but now in what John considers the normal Christian state of heart.

then have we confidence toward God

See on 2.28. Here the original sense of *parrhēsia*, ' plain speaking ', is to the fore. The freedom of the father-child relation in intercourse is its picture of the Christian at prayer. Its archetype is the *parrhēsia* of Christ with him whom he addressed as ' *Abba* '.

In Christian prayer, all barriers are down, all fears cast

aside. The true children, at home in their Father's presence,
may say—and ask (v. 22)—what comes from the heart.

22. . . . and whatsoever we ask we receive of him

Cp. Mark 11.24. Not really a 'blank cheque' for our
petitions. (*a*) The assurance is given in the setting of this
open-hearted, 'true'-hearted speaking to God which is the
sincere Christian's privilege. Brooke makes the point well.
'All requests are granted *which can be put forward in the
freedom of intercourse which has been described.*'[1] More
explicitly, (*b*) John's assurance is given on the assumption
that we keep God's commands and do what pleases him
(v. 22b). (Cp. James 5.16.) If these considerable conditions
are met, we shall ask aright and be answered. See 5.14 f.
and notes.

23. . . . believe on the name of his Son Jesus Christ, and love one another

Lit., 'give credence to the name of . . .' The construction is *pisteuein* and dative. Contrast with *pisteuein eis*,
e.g. I John 5.10 or John 6.29, 'believe in him whom he has
sent', i.e. 'give personal devotion to . . .', may be over-
drawn. This is true especially here, when we recall that a
man's NAME meant to the biblical writers almost 'person'.
His NAME summed up his whole nature and character as
revealed in word and action. (Cp. Ps. 124.8.) To BELIEVE
ON THE NAME OF HIS SON JESUS CHRIST is to accept
as true all that Jesus Christ is and has done and stands
for.

The commandment is twofold—'believing on the name'
and brotherly love.[2] Note that the theme of true belief (and
false) is developed in 4.1-6 and again in 5.4b-21; that of
true brotherly love in 4.7-5.4a.

[1] Brooke, p. 102: our italics.
[2] For the necessary connection between faith and love, cp. Gal. 5.6.

38544

23b. as he gave us commandment

In vv. 22 and 23a HIS COMMANDMENT(S) are clearly commandments of *God*. Now, in the closing phrase of v. 23, HE
is Christ and the giving of the COMMANDMENT that of John
13.34 or 15.12.

24a. ' In simple obedience to the commands of God (of
Christ) we recognise the reality of that intimate union
between God and His children which is described as a
mutual indwelling ' (Dodd). Cp. John 15.7-10. John is insist-
ing, as always (cp. 2.6 ff., 24-29), that abiding in the light,
or in God or Christ, is no mere mystical experience. It is
inseparable from down-to-earth ethical obedience, i.e.
' doing the truth ' in sincere practical love, together with
sound Gospel belief.

24b. *Your Spirit his confirming gift*

The closing clause of v. 24, BY THE SPIRIT WHICH HE
HATH GIVEN US, is yet a third ' swing-door '. It leads into the
new matter of 4.1-6. But it also links the new with the
old.

The Spirit, John says, confirms indwelling by God (3.24b).
But of whom? Surely those—just in mind—who keep his
COMMANDMENTS of true belief and love (vv. 22 f.). THE
SPIRIT meant in 3.24 is the gift of God *to those who
belong to the truth, and prove in practice that they
do.*

As earlier, John is at pains here to reassure his readers
about their Christian standing. We may imagine some
who interrupt v. 24 to say: ' Yes, we do sincerely try to
keep his commandments and we *hope* God abides in us and
we in him, but how can we be *sure* we do? ' John points
them to the Spirit's witness in their hearts: God's own gifted
confirmation.

As soon as he says SPIRIT, however, he realises that before
THE SPIRIT can be effective reassurance for them he has to

clarify and warn—that not all is gold that spiritually glisters! This he does in 4.1-6.

4.1-6. *Your Spirit—of God and of truth*

There is, John knows well, another, contrary, 'spirit' abroad, from a very different source and in men to match— viz., the heretical false prophets (vv. 1, 3). Verses 1-6 say, in effect: 'Look out! Not "any and every" (NEB) spirit is the *Holy* Spirit. Test for source (v. 1). The criterion is acceptance or rejection of fundamental Gospel truth.[1] The " spirit " in men who hold true belief (v. 2) and acknowledge it when they hear it from others (cp. v. 6a) is therefore the Spirit of God. Theirs is the very Spirit of truth; and they themselves are " of God " (v. 6). To reject true belief and those who voice it, on the other hand, reveals men as not " of God " but " of the world ". Their " spirit " is that not of God but Antichrist, not of truth but error (cp. vv. 3, 6).'

The passage certainly shows up the heretics. But also it reassures, while it warns, the orthodox. Its force to them we take to be: 'Be assured, you are of God.[2] *His* Spirit is yours (3.24). Never forget, however, that it *is* the Spirit of God and, at the same time, of *truth* (4.6). Possession of his Spirit is dependent upon your *true confession*, " that Jesus Christ is come in the flesh " (v. 2).'

1. Believe not every spirit

The Spirit, from Pentecost on, was the Christian's normal, expected possession. The New Testament records public signs of Spirit-possession such as ecstatic speaking with (strange) tongues at worship (e.g. I Cor. 14). It also speaks of prophecy (I Cor. 14: cp. also I Cor. 12.28 f.) as a spiritual gift some members—prophets—have: preaching

[1] Specifically, 'that Jesus Christ is come in the flesh' (v. 2).
[2] In v. 4 and v. 6, the Greek pronouns YE and WE are emphatic, contrasted with the equally emphatic THEY in v. 5.

of an intelligible, if also (we gather) often emotionally super-charged, kind.

This gift of prophecy 'in the spirit'—highly honoured in the Church[1]—posed for John, in his care of the Asian churches, a grave problem. 'What are you to make of men obviously "in the spirit"—*some* spirit—who prophesy things in flat contradiction to basic Christian doctrine?' John's answer is that these are false prophets (4.1, as foretold in e.g. Mark 13.22; cp. also Deut. 13.1-5). 'Inspiration', however evident, is *per se* no criterion of truth. The real test is what inspiration leads men to say.[2] 'Jesus is the Christ come in the flesh' is cardinal Christian truth. It needs the Spirit of truth and of God to declare it (4.2). To deny it 'in the spirit' shows the spirit to be that of error (4.6), of antichrist (4.3b)—and not at all of God (4.3a; cp. I Cor. 12.3). So John warns: 'Stop giving credence to spirits indiscriminately. Put them to the test.' (Note that 'discerning of spirits' [I Cor. 12.10] was itself a recognised spiritual gift.)

because many false prophets are gone out into the world

The urgent reason for applying the test. Those who had 'gone out' (2.19) from the Church into pagan society to spread their heresies apparently enjoyed much prestige as spiritual men. John says: 'Even so, they are *false* prophets —recognise them as such!'

2. Hereby know ye

Probably indicative (RSV), not imperative.

Every spirit that confesseth that Jesus Christ is come in the flesh

AV and RSV rather obscure the exact intention of the

---

[1] In I Cor. 12.29 the prophets are listed next to the apostles. See also on 'the brethren' in III John; pp. 162 ff.

[2] And do. Cp. *Didache* 11.8: 'Not every one who speaks in a spirit is a prophet; he is only a prophet if he walks in the ways of the Lord.'

Greek: lit., 'Every spirit which confesses Jesus Christ having come in the flesh.' *Note*: (1) 'confesses' has a *personal*,
not propositional, object; (2) in interpretation we have to
choose between (a) 'confesses Jesus, the Christ who has
come in the flesh' and (b) 'confesses Jesus Christ, who has
come in the flesh'. We prefer (a), and Moffatt's rendering,
'confesses Jesus as the Christ Incarnate'. Both assert, anti-
docetically, the *really* incarnate Jesus; (a) asserts more
specifically that the Divine Christ 'became flesh' and was
essentially one with Jesus. (See notes on 2.22 and 5.6.) The
best reading of v. 3 supports our preference.

3. And every spirit that confesseth not that Jesus Christ is come in the flesh

Read (with RSV and Moffatt): 'and every spirit which
does not confess Jesus'. AV follows texts into which words
from v. 2 have intruded.

confesseth not

An interesting variant *luei*—giving 'every spirit which
separates (or divides) Jesus'—stood in the Greek text of
Irenaeus, Origen and Clement. It probably crept in to make
the condemnation apply more clearly to some Cerinthian-
style heresy of their time.

this is that spirit of antichrist . . .

NEB is excellent: 'This is what is meant by "Antichrist"; you have been told that he was to come, and here
he is, in the world already!' Here, as in 2.18, 21 f., Antichrist is essentially 'lie' and rejection of truth—notably
truth about Christ's Person. Cp. II John 7.

4-6a. Ye are of God . . . he that is not of God heareth not us

The need of these verses[1] is further sign of the heretics'

[1] Almost in parenthesis, between v. 3 and v. 6b.

power and readers' diffidence. They counter two reactions
John takes his vv. 1-3 to have provoked from his readers:
(*a*) a timorous cry, 'Yes, we know they have the spirit of
Antichrist, but they are so strong and so successful!'; and
(*b*) a painful question, 'If we are of God, as you say we are,
why does the world reject our message and yet heed the
heretics?'

Verses 4-6a, freely paraphrased and elaborated, reply:

(*a*) 'Don't be afraid of them. You do belong to God (v. 4)—
and because of that (since God in you is greater than the
devil in the heretics) "you have the mastery" (NEB) over
them.[1] Yet

(*b*) Don't be surprised (cp. 3.13) at the reception the world
gives you—and the heretics. They belong to the world
(v. 5); they speak its language and the world listens to them.
You are quite different. You belong to God. The man who
knows God will listen to you (v. 6a) but expect no responsive hearing from anyone else.' (Cp. John 15.18 f.)

4. greater is he that is in you

God or the Spirit of God. It is tempting but probably
wrong to find allusion here to John 16.33 and the idea that
Christ (who has 'overcome the world') in Christians assures
and makes over to them his victory.

6a. We are of God: he that knoweth God heareth us: he that is not of God heareth not us

Isolated, these statements could end missionary effort
towards those indifferent and hostile to our message.
(Rather smugly assured, too, they are, about the perfection
of the manner in which 'we' have presented it!) In over-
simplifying the issues, John 'has expressed himself somewhat incautiously'.[2] Yet—give him his due—he has faced

[1] By having remained true, despite heretical onslaughts, to the original
Christian Gospel, they had proved this. Cp. also 2.13 f.
[2] Dodd, p. 101.

up to this perennially baffling question raised by missionary experience: Why do some people stubbornly reject Gospel truth which others accept? We find unsatisfactory, dangerous even, his answer that—by predestination?—men are ultimately divided into those who know God and therefore will heed Christians, and those who do not belong to him and therefore will not and cannot. Yet we are left with the facts—that 'in spite of all complications and obfuscations, men do come face to face with the truth, and . . . range themselves by their response to it'.[1] And for an answer to 'Why?'—other than John's? We can but say with Dodd, 'For ultimate reasons . . . which we cannot penetrate.'[2]

6b. Hereby

Not only by the rule given in v. 6a, but by truth-acceptance or truth-denial as the test of spirits throughout vv. 1-6.

GOD IS LOVE

4.7–5.4a

The third main division now opens. It is the best-known and best-loved portion of the Epistle: a passage with good claim to be set—without shame—alongside I Cor. 13. John has prepared his readers carefully for it. First in 'Light implies love' (2.3–2.17), then in 'Life implies love' (3.11–3.19a), he has shown that light and life are only vapid, indeed potentially dangerous, terms, unless interpreted by love. Now the focus is directly upon love itself—the love of God for man, and of man for God and his brother.

[1] *Ibid.*, p. 102.
[2] *Ibid.*

Essay II: GOD IS LOVE (4.8, 16)

In this section John rises to his greatest theological affirmation.[1] He stopped short of making it even in his Gospel, the profoundest book in the New Testament. No other New Testament writer ever attains to it. No one in any age could ever surpass it. 'God is love.'

Twice he says it, in 4.8 and 4.16. The repetition suggests to us not only John's own underlining of the fact that 'God is love' is the motif which controls this whole section's argument, but his own awe and wonder at the sublimity of the truth captured at last in these simplest of words. He can't get away from it, as it were.

Our danger is to underestimate the phrase's content. At two points we must take particular care: (1) the meaning of the term 'love', and (2) the meaning rightly to be attached to saying of God that he 'is love'. (1) The term *agapē* has been sufficiently treated under 3.16a.[2] It is necessary only to recall here, that *agapē* means 'all give', that its primary reference is to *God's* love (and only thereafter—derivatively—extended to describe the Christian's love) and that its 'colour' of 'all give' comes from the supreme demonstration of love in the gift and life and death of Jesus Christ. This giving without limit, indifferent alike to self-interest and to the merit of the beloved—this is the 'love' which 'God is'.

(2) 'God *is* love'. The form is that of an abstract proposition. Study of the analogous 'God is light',[3] however, cautions us that even Hellenistic-sounding phrases from John's pen originate in a Jewish-Christian mind. Such a

---

[1] Dodd's pp. 106-110 on 'God is love' are among the finest even he has written. To his insights here we are specially indebted in what follows.

[2] See pp. 92-94.

[3] See Essay I, pp. 46 f.

mind never thought in abstractions. Alien to it, for example, was Hellenistic thought which, even at its most developed, was of God as impersonal deity, absolute Being. To John, as all in the Hebraic-Christian tradition, God was fully personal and dynamic; always acting, always the *living* God.

For John, therefore, *what God is* is learned by *what God does*. What does he do? No list could comprehend his deeds. What really matters is that we know the central act of all God's activity to be his sending of his Kingdom, in sending Christ. How are we to characterise that divine action? 'The answer given in the Fourth Gospel is: *God loved the world so dearly that He gave up His only son . . .*' (John 3.16, to which I John 4.9 alludes). Dodd continues: [1] 'The coming of His Kingdom is an act of love. Hence, if we ask, what is God's nature? the answer must be given in terms of love.' So John arrives at 'God is love'.

Note two important points. *First:* we see now (what the form obscured) that behind John's 'God is love' stands conviction of a personal God whose known acts in history have shown him 'to be love'. John's 'God is love' is thus worlds removed from 'God is Love' (with a capital 'L'). The latter abstract metaphysical notion an Hellenistic philosopher or mystery-religionist might have conceived: John, never!

And, *secondly:* 'God is love' is richer far in meaning than merely 'God is loving' or 'God loves'. These phrases could mean that 'loving' was only one of God's many activities; that, e.g., creating, ruling, judging were as characteristic of him; that at times he was not 'loving' but something else. But 'God is love', we saw, is based on the belief that God's supreme, and supremely *characteristic*, action is his 'loving' in the gift of Christ. So '"God is love"' implies that *all* his activity is loving activity. If he creates, he creates in love; if he rules, he rules in love: if he judges,

[1] *Dodd*, p. 108.

he judges in love. All that he does is the expression of his nature, which is—to love.'[1]

Much spiritual malaise (as well as theological error) would be avoided if the truth of this were acknowledged; if, in particular, the wrath and judgment of God were considered in its light. Their *modus operandi* remains hard to fathom but so much is clear. If God is love, they must be neither opposed to, nor even merely co-existent with, but *contained within*, the love of God. God is love through and through.[2] He can do nothing whatever which does not have the texture of love.

We sub-divide 4.7–5.4a thus:

4.7-12	The Origin of Love and its Response
4.13-19	The Assurance of Love
4.20–5.4a	The Test of Love

7-12. *The Origin of Love and its Response*

LET US LOVE ONE ANOTHER (v. 7). Why? Because love and its practitioners—they alone—belong to God. Why so? Because 'God *is* love' (v. 8). How do we know? Because God has shown himself to be love in sending Christ to be the means of our forgiveness—and our 'life' (vv. 9 f.). Make no mistake! This is how we know God and know what love is; not by any passionate yearning, on our initiative, after *him* but by his actual given demonstration of love for *us* (v. 10). That is why we should love one another—as response to his shown love for us (v. 11). How important, however, this response is! Only by it is God 'seen' on earth, when seen to indwell us as his love appears in our visible acts of brotherly love (v. 12).

7. Let us love one another

These words, beginning the new division, pick up 3.23b,

[1] Dodd, p. 110.
[2] Cp. 1.5: ' In him is no darkness at all.'

AND LOVE ONE ANOTHER . . ., for development. No less than 29 instances of *agapaō*, or its derivatives, occur in the next 15 verses. John is 'rapt' in love.

9. Practically John 3.16. MANIFESTED . . . TOWARD US mistranslates *en hēmin*. Better, 'manifested among us' or simply 'disclosed to us' (NEB).

10. Herein is love, not that we loved God, but that he loved us

Cp. v. 19. The primacy and initiative of God's love are strongly affirmed. In contrast, consider Hellenistic religion. In it, God, being passionless, could not love man. In it man loved God in the sense of yearning, as a finite creature, after the Infinite. This non-Christian, man-initiated 'love' is *erōs*, of course: Christian love is *agapē*, and it is God's before it is ours.

12a. No man hath seen God at any time

Cp. John 1.18. In both cases regard HATH SEEN as in inverted commas. John glances at those in the Greek world (his heretics included) who claimed to 'see' God through mystic rites and rapture. True to the Hebraic mind,[1] he thought little of 'the direct, mystical vision of God as a goal of religious aspiration in this life'.[2] But both in John 1 and here he vehemently asserts, in almost the same breath, that God has in fact been seen—in Christ Incarnate (John 1.14, 18; 14.9; I John 1.2, cp. 4.14) and also thus, in the loving deeds of those in whom God dwells (4.12).

[1] 'In Hebrew religion hearing, not seeing, is the key to religious experience' (Dodd, p. 112). On this theme, we commend also the absorbing book: *Hebrew Thought Compared with Greek*, by Thorleif Boman, tr. J. Moreau, SCM Press, 1960.
[2] Dodd, p. 113.

12b. Our mutual love is the outward visible sign of God dwelling in us, Thus, too, his love for us is 'brought to perfection within us' (NEB). God's love, seen in us when it 'follows through' into love of the brethren, lets the invisible God be seen.

13-19. *The Assurance of Love*

Are we sure that we really have this mutual indwelling of God and us? (*a*) The gift of the Spirit, remember (3.24), assures us (4.13). (*b*) Further: we have seen (v. 14) the coming of Jesus the Incarnate Son sent as the world's Saviour. We openly profess this conviction. We live, therefore, in consuming awareness of God's love (v. 16a). But GOD IS LOVE, so to dwell in love's realm is to dwell in God (vv. 15 f.). (*c*) A further point. We have in Christ one perfectly indwelling the Father (v. 17b). We even in this world are like Christ in this—with God's love for us and ours for him and our brother a reality completely possessing us. Then not fear—for love excludes it—but boldness is ours on Judgment Day (vv. 17 f.).

We doubt if our love for God is so 'perfect' as that? (*d*) Remember (v. 10a) the ground of our love and capacity to love: nothing of *our* doing but God's. At the last, *this* is our real assurance—his sure, shown, prior love for us, not ours for him.

13. Note that though John returns to his statement of 3.24 (now clarified by 4.1-6), he still does not dwell on the Spirit but hastens to safer, more objective ground (vv. 14-16) for his readers' assurance.

14. A fair summary of the whole Gospel.

15. confess that Jesus is the Son of God

This is almost certainly a citation of an ancient Church

creed, as found in the Western reading in Acts 8.37, incorporated in AV.[1]

16. And we have known and believed the love that God hath to us

John's readers who with the whole Church have seen and made public witness to the Gospel events (vv. 14 f.) have seen therein, and testify to, above all, the *love* of God. (So vv. 7-10 made plain.) Claimed by God's love which they have come to know (cp. John 6.69, 'be sure of') and believe, they can be said to 'dwell in love'.

he that dwelleth in love

Take LOVE comprehensively, as love by God, love for God, love for the brother. Paraphrase, perhaps, simply by 'he who continues to live in the sphere of love'—that in which God's love is acknowledged as 'the greatest thing in the world' and responsive love directs all human action.

dwelleth in God

He must be at one with God, for love is God's very own *habitat*.

17. Herein is our love made perfect, that we may have boldness

This verse is grammatically perplexing. (*a*) Does HEREIN look forward to THAT WE MAY HAVE BOLDNESS? Then, the words mean: 'With us love finds its peak (Barclay) in this fact, that we have full confidence on Judgment Day.' (*b*) Or, does HEREIN look back (less usual in John) to v. 16b? That is: 'In this mutual fellowship, love with us finds its consummation; as a result[2] we have absolute confidence. . . .'

---

[1] Given in the margin of RV and as a footnote in NEB. See O. Cullmann, *Christology of the New Testament*, Eng. trs., SCM Press, 1959, p. 291.

[2] *hina*, as often, to express result rather than purpose.

PERFECT LOVE CASTETH OUT FEAR (v. 18), and 2.28 (closely
parallel to 4.17) seem to favour (b). It gets our verdict. See
note on 2.28.

in the day of judgment

Notable exponent of realised eschatology though John is,
he retains belief in a final Day of reckoning. (See note on
2.18.) With other New Testament writers, he was wrong in
believing that it would be soon, but right in stressing its
certainty, its nature (for our weal or woe) as shaped by our
alignments (e.g. light, life, love, truth or their opposites)
now, and the urgency which the impending Day gives to
daily life.

John's immediate point here is: life 'in love' means life
'in God'; such life of mutual fellowship here and now
means a fearless Doomsday.

because as he is, so are we in this world

As usual AS HE IS (cp. 3.3, 5 etc.; see note on 3.7) refers
to the 'whole human Christ', Exalted as well as Incarnate.
Jesus and the Father are mutually indwelling (cp. John
14.10 f. etc.) in perfect love and fellowship. This relationship is the archetype of ours with God. Jesus could never
be thought to 'fear' the Father. The Christian, in like
relationship now, can only be fearless before God, even on
Judgment Day.

18. There is no fear in love

In LOVE, divine-human as well as human, FEAR—except,
as Dodd remarks, the 'fear of hurting one another' and
'fear of affronting the love of God'—has no place. When
the relationship of mutual love is perfect it 'drives all dread
away' (Moffatt). What if we still do fear? Our love for God
is less than complete. Something mars it. (The likely trouble
[see vv. 20 f.] is our failure to love our brother—vital if our
love of God is to be complete and our fellowship with him
free from fear.)

Fear hath torment

'Fear brings with it the pains of judgment' (NEB). Imperfection in love carries fear of punishment in the judgment. The Greek suggests the fearful pain of anticipated punishment as itself part of the punishment. John does not linger on this thought. For Christians who truly live in love, dread is gone and, with it, 'pains of judgment'.

19. We love him because he first loved us

AV (probably influenced by v. 10) misleads in supplying HIM to the objectless Greek verb. Read: 'We love because he loved us first.' Only by God's prior love of us do we know what love is and have the capacity for loving (anyone, God and brother alike). Though close in thought to v. 10, the verse is freshened by its new context of assurance for Judgment Day. This, then, is our ultimate security, says John: love's source in God's initiative, our being loved by him.

4.20-5.4a. *The Test of Love*

How is our love for God proved *real*? By practical love shown to our brother. Suppose we say 'We love God' and yet we hate our brother, we are liars. Our 'love' is unreal. Love for God without love for men is a moral impossibility. So, if we are to love God, brotherly love is no *option* (v. 20). Remember, too: brotherly love (as well as love to God) is God's explicit *command!* (v. 21). Yet another point. We who believe 'Jesus is the Christ' are children of God. We love the Father. Consistency demands that we love *his* as well as *him*; 'love the Father' has its necessary corollary 'love the child'—our brother-child of the same loved Father. When we see our rebirth as into a *family*, obedient *filial* love is seen to include, automatically, *fraternal* love (5.1 f.).

To sum up: to love God is simply to keep his command-

H

ments. 'Simply?' Are they not beyond keeping? No. Exacting they are, but not burdensome. Their demand can be
met, for the divine quality of life given us in our rebirth
overcomes all obstacles (5.3-4a).

20. If a man say, I love God and hateth his brother . . .

Cp. 2.4-11 and 3.10b-18 for earlier treatment of this
heresy held by the seceders. Now John is thinking more
generally of anyone deluded by his emotions of 'love' into
confident assertion that he loves God. Deluded, because his
feelings permit him actually to hate his brother. His profession is a lie. He cannot love God if his action contradicts
brotherly love.

he that loveth not his brother whom he hath seen, how can he love God whom he hath not seen?

Read (with RSV and NEB): '. . . cannot love God
. . .' Do not interpret as 'Success claimed in the greater
task is denied by failure in the smaller.' For our author,
'love for God' and 'love for the brethren' are not separate
tasks or different stages of difficulty in learning to love. His
whole contention (vv. 11 f., 21) is the indissolubility of the
love-God-and-brother obligation. Where brotherly love is
visibly lacking, love for God must be lacking too. The
'cannot'—*ou dynatai*—expresses moral impossibility, not
spiritual immaturity. Scott Easton writes, with grace as well
as truth: 'God has set our brother where we can see him
in order to give our love an object; if we neglect this object
which stands before us, there is no profit in proclaiming
our love of an invisible God, for without love of man love
of God cannot exist.'[1]

21. And this commandment have we from him

It is a COMMANDMENT, and given by God. To disobey him

[1] B. Scott Easton, 'The Letters of John', *Abingdon Bible Commentary*,
p. 1356.

(by hating the brother) accords ill with claims to love him. Although the conjunction of 'love God' and 'love your brother' is not actually made in Jesus' Fourth Gospel teaching, John seems to know traditional teaching such as Mark's 'love the Lord thy God . . . and . . . thy neighbour as thyself' (Mark 12.28-31).

5.1. Whosoever believeth . . . is born of God . . . him also that is begotten of him

John appears to pick up the phrase 'his brother' which closes ch. 4, reflect upon it, and find it apt to illuminate further the error of the 'liar' of 4.20. His mental preface to 5.1 might be: 'Doesn't the man see what "his brother" means? "His brother" is "his own Father's son". How can he profess love for his Father and hate a child who also belongs to his Father? Not without a "lie".' 5.1 itself means 'Every Christian[1] is a child of God'; and 'love the father, love his child' is a universally-acknowledged principle, which applies to the Christian. The saying of v. 1b is, of course, almost a proverb. It applies to *any* family. John exploits it in application to the family of God.

2. By this *(en toutō)* we know

As, e.g., in 3.19; 4.17, John probably intends BY THIS to glance backwards to v. 1. (So also Dodd, against Moffatt and Brooke.) That is: 'Because of this "love me, love my child" principle in human society, "it follows that" (NEB) when we in the Christian family love God our Father . . . we love his children, our fellow-Christian brothers.' In God's family, as any other, a truly loving son is bound to be a loving brother.

3. For this is the love of God, that we keep his commandments

This takes up AND KEEP HIS COMMANDMENTS, added as a

---

[1] i.e. 'whosoever believeth that Jesus is the Christ'—the basic Christian belief, for Jew and Gentile alike.

kind of afterthought to v. 2; and resumes the thought of
4.21, of the relatedness of love and obedience. There the
idea was that love is not love which disobeys the beloved's
commands; here, that love to God *means*—or consists in—
obedience to his commands.

3b-4a. his commandments are not grievous

Lit. 'heavy'. John imagines a reader saying 'But this
obedience is impossibly hard!' and quickly writes 5.3-4a
for his comfort. Verse 3b surely echoes Christ: 'My yoke
is easy, and my burden is light (Matt. 11.30).' It does not
mean that God's commands are effortlessly simple to fulfil.
(The demands of the Sermon on the Mount are hardly
child's play!) Rather, they are not irksome or burdensome.
Why? Partly, no doubt, because God does not demand
what is too hard for men.[1] More specifically, because
WHATEVER IS BORN OF GOD, OVERCOMETH THE WORLD (4a).
Every Christian 'has within himself a power', that of his
new birth from God, 'strong enough to overcome the resistance of all the powers of the world, which hinder him from
loving God',[2] i.e. from keeping his commandments (v. 3).

THE TRUE GOD

5.4b-21

Division of opinion over the analysis of I John 5 is sharp.
Most commentators conclude that v. 13 ends the letter
proper, the rest being 'epilogue', 'postscript'. They do so
largely because of the close parallel of v. 13 to John 20.31,

---

[1] Cp. I Cor. 10.13 (NEB): 'God keeps faith, and he will not allow
you to be tested above your powers, but when the test comes he will at
the same time provide a way out, by enabling you to sustain it.'

[2] Brooke, p. 130.

close enough to be called conscious reminiscence. But whereas ch. 21 is not integral to the Fourth Gospel, and is a true 'Appendix', vv. 14-21 of the Epistle, we believe (here we are in a minority with Robert Law), belong to its substance and conclude its argument.

So we make the letter's final main division 5.4b-21. As a title, 'True Belief' or 'The Truth' would not be wrong. We think best, however, 'The True God' (v. 20).

We make the following sub-divisions:

5-6a.	The content of true belief
4b, 6b-12.	The blessings of true belief
13-20.	The certainties of true belief
21.	Final warning

This closing division is very markedly devoted to meeting the needs of John's beloved little children, diffident and heresy-harassed. It first emphasises the victory which is their Christian title, and makes precise the doctrines which are essential Christian truth. It ends with the declaration of a series of ringing Christian certainties which his truly believing readers (he can remind them) *know* they enjoy. The letter's final word is a challenge: 'Stay true! You have the true God and you know you have—and all those glorious certainties besides. Then steer clear of "idols"!'

THE CONTENT OF TRUE BELIEF

5.5-6a

(1) *Jesus* is *the Son of God* (v. 5)

he that believeth that Jesus is the Son of God
Cp. 2.22; 4.15, and (with the same meaning) 5.1, WHO-
SOEVER BELIEVETH THAT JESUS IS THE CHRIST. John means

belief that the Divine Christ or Divine Son of God was Incarnate in Jesus. (Denial of this, we recall, characterised
the Docetic heretics.) Belief in the real Incarnation of the
Divine Christ—the Christian hallmark (v. 1)—is, says John,
indispensable for victory over the world.

John is right. Only an uncompromising doctrine of the
Incarnation assures us that we have really seen *God*, and
that his love is no wishful dream but truth—surely and his-
torically manifested. This taken away, the godless world is
victor. But this faith makes all faith strong and the believer
invincible.[1]

(2) *Jesus* Christ *was crucified* (v. 6a)

Thus we attempt to define the doctrinal point specified in
THIS IS HE THAT CAME BY WATER AND BLOOD, EVEN JESUS
CHRIST; NOT BY WATER ONLY, BUT BY WATER AND BLOOD. So
AV, RV, RSV, NEB. Rightly, despite two excellent MSS
which read: 'This is he that came by water and blood and
Spirit' (cp. the trio in v. 8).

What does it mean to call Jesus Christ him THAT CAME BY
WATER AND BLOOD? Note first the title JESUS CHRIST. In I
John, 'Christ' means Divine Son of God; 'pre-existent'
Christ would convey, for today, its meaning here. Next:
the phrase HE THAT CAME (*ho elthōn*). The Greek makes the
'coming' refer to a definite historical event. The 'coming'
of Christ the Son corresponds to the 'sending' of the
Father (cp. 4.9 and Fourth Gospel, *passim*). The Greek
definite article in HE THAT CAME makes WHO CAME BY WATER
AND BLOOD characterise Christ's mission.[2] The importance
of these points is that they clearly show that CAME BY WATER
AND BLOOD must refer to specific events in Christ's Incarnate
experience, events notably defining his work's character.

[1] See below on 'The Blessings of True Belief': v. 4b: (1) Experience
of Victory.

[2] See Brooke, p. 134.

Two common interpretations thus fall short, that the water and the blood (1) primarily refer to the flow of water and blood from the side of Christ Crucified (John 19.34), or (2) allude to the two sacraments of Baptism and the Eucharist.[1] BY WATER is 'through the event of his baptism by John the Baptist'; AND BLOOD is 'through the event of the Crucifixion'. In the former, Jesus Christ was consecrated to his work; in the latter, his work was consummated. Together they sum up his 'coming'.

For lucidity, we have separated vv. 5 and 6a for discussion. In fact v. 6a flows out of v. 5. It defines more closely the belief of v. 5: JESUS IS THE SON OF GOD. It says in effect: 'Yes, the Divine Christ came in Jesus (cp. v. 5) and his coming was signally characterised by the two historical events of his Baptism and his death on the Cross.'

This is not quite all. John adds: NOT BY WATER ONLY, BUT BY WATER AND BLOOD. Great weight is thus thrown on the words AND BLOOD. Some must have been saying that Jesus Christ *did* come by water but not by *blood*. What heresy is this? Probably Cerinthianism. Cerinthus[2] taught as follows. At the baptism the Divine Christ came into the man Jesus. Jesus, allied now to the Divine Christ, brought news of the hitherto unknown God and lived and ministered in perfect virtue. Just before the Crucifixion the Christ left Jesus and returned to glory. The man Jesus was crucified and resurrected.

This view accepted Christ's coming 'by water'; it denied (since for no Gnostic could the Divine suffer) Christ's coming 'by blood', the blood of the Cross. John's seceding teachers seem to have been tarred with this Cerinthian brush. In v. 6a he leaves his readers in no doubt about where orthodox Christianity stands. The Christ and Jesus were one Jesus Christ, on the Cross as throughout the ministry. Jesus *Christ* was crucified! To believe this is vital. The Cerinthian

[1] For discussion see Brooke, pp. 132-136.
[2] Barclay, pp. 126 f. See also pp. 35 f. above.

teaching 'robs . . . the death of Jesus of all value for us.
By seeking to protect God from all contact with human
pain . . . it removes God from the act of redemption and
empties the Cross of its value.'[1] BY BLOOD (real blood,
really *his* blood) is the essence of how, in fact, God 'came'
in Jesus Christ—and the very nub of our assurance of
Atonement.

THE BLESSINGS OF TRUE BELIEF

5.4b, 6b-12

(1) *Experience of Victory* (v. 4b)

This is the victory that overcometh the world, even our faith
    Moffatt preserves the Greek word-play (*hē nikē hē
nikēsasa*) by ' the conquest which conquers'. See above (on
vv. 5-6a) how John goes on to define this FAITH. It is belief,
in short, in Jesus Christ really Incarnate, really Crucified—
and this not only ' as an intellectual conviction but as a rule
of life'.[2] This FAITH it is which gives THE VICTORY THAT
OVERCOMETH. The Greek aorist, *nikēsasa*, obscured in AV,
hints at a definite moment of *nikē*. The moment of each
Christian's conversion? As probably, the time when those
addressed, though greatly drawn to follow the seceders
' into the world', had found power to stay loyal. See note
on 4.4.

(2) *The Assured Authenticity of True Belief* (vv. 6b-12)

    Within these verses occur several references, best con-
sidered together, to witness borne to the truth of Christian

[1] Barclay, p. 126.
[2] Brooke, p. 131.

doctrine. Testimony, always of special interest to John,[1] has here great practical value. By pointing to various witnesses to the authenticity of their sound belief John intends to dispel his readers' notable diffidence.

6b. And it is the Spirit that beareth witness, because the Spirit is truth

In the New Testament 'the chief function of the Spirit is to bear witness to Christ (John 15.26; 16.13-15) or . . . to the truth (alētheia), for Christ is truth (John 14.6).'[2] The Spirit is the Spirit of truth (John 16.13; cp. I John 4.6). Indeed, says John here, 'the Spirit *is* the truth' (RSV; Greek, hē alētheia).

We interpret thus. The Spirit it is which bears witness to Jesus Christ having come BY WATER AND BLOOD (v. 6a), because the very nature of the Spirit is truth. 'By its very nature it is not only capable of bearing true witness, but it is also constrained to do so. It cannot deny itself.'[3] The present tense BEARETH WITNESS precludes *limitation* of reference to the Spirit's testimony at the Baptism (Mark 1.11) and before the Passion (John 12.28); it emphasises the Paraclete's continuing witness in the Church to Christ and his coming by water and by blood. Cp. John 14.26; 15.26; 16.7 ff., 13-15.

7. For there are three that bear record in heaven, the Father, the Word, and the Holy Ghost: and these three are one

A spurious interpolation, read by AV. This is a fourth-century gloss, written into the Latin version, probably in Spain,[4] which became the authorised Latin text, and then

[1] See the Fourth Gospel, especially John 5.19-47.
[2] A. Richardson, *An Introduction to the Theology of the New Testament*, SCM Press, 1958, p. 112.
[3] Brooke, p. 136.
[4] Because first quoted as I John by Priscillian, the Spanish heretic (died AD 385).

was translated and interpolated into Greek texts. It entered English editions through the Greek Textus Receptus which AV translated.[1]

8. And there are three that bear witness in earth, the spirit, and the water, and the blood: and these three agree in one

Disregard IN EARTH, not in the Greek text. THESE THREE AGREE IN ONE is lit. 'are for the one thing'. They have a common purpose. Read directly after v. 6, v. 8 is reasonably clear. Both THE WATER and THE BLOOD, i.e. the Baptism and the Cross, bear witness to the character of Christ and his mission. The third witness, supreme in importance and mentioned already in v. 6b, is THE SPIRIT. 'The Spirit is *the* witness-bearer' (because not only past but present—see on v. 6), 'to what the Christ was and came to do.'[2] Above all, the witnesses AGREE. The force of the final clause derives from Jewish law in which a fact had to be proved before two or three witnesses (Deut. 19.15). The threefold consentient witness to Jesus, in all that the Church holds him to be, satisfies legal demands for valid attestation.

9. For this is the witness of God which he hath testified of his Son

Follow NEB: 'And this threefold testimony is indeed that of God Himself, the witness he has borne to his Son.'

Three points are distinguishable in v. 9. (1) The testimony to Christ of water, blood and Spirit is, in a true appraisal, *God* speaking; God bearing witness. (2) We accept human evidence (9a):[3] *a fortiori* Divine witness must surely have our even readier acceptance. (3) This Divine witness is that of God himself concerning his *Son*.

---

[1] For greater detail, see Dodd's comprehensive footnote, pp. 127 f.
[2] Brooke, p. 136.
[3] As e.g. in Jewish legal practice, just alluded to in v. 8.

Any father's witness to his son has special claim to acceptance. In the unique case of the Divine-human Son—where even the best purely human witness to him can only be 'true as far as it goes'—witness of the Divine is invaluable, and witness of the Divine *Father* concerning *his own Son* represents the very acme of reliability.

10. He that believeth on the Son of God hath the witness in himself

To John's impressive list of witnesses authenticating true belief—THE SPIRIT, THE SPIRIT in agreement with THE WATER and THE BLOOD, the Divine Father testifying concerning his own Son—he adds this last; the confirming witness in the heart—the *testimonium spiritus internum*—granted to the true believer as he goes on living his life personally committed in trust and obedience to Christ. Such is the kind of ' believing' meant by BELIEVETH ON (*pisteuein eis*). In marked contrast here (though not in 3.23) is BE-LIEVETH (*pisteuein* with dative) in v. 10b: HE THAT BELIEV-ETH NOT GOD.

Far from having committed his whole life to God, this man does not even accept God's word of testimony as true. Such men—the heretical seceders, for example—make God a liar, ' accusing the Truth of falsehood' (Dodd)! 'What could be greater blasphemy than actually to disbelieve God's witness concerning his own Son? '[1]

11. And this is the record

Here and in v. 10 RECORD is *martyria*, ' witness', exactly as in v. 9.

God hath given to us eternal life

Earlier, John has described the witness to Christ in its characteristics: now he defines its essential content. With

---

[1] Thus we try to bring out the force of the last part of v. 10, which repeats, almost to the letter, the closing words of v. 9.

John's definition cp. 'I am come that they might have life
. . . more abundantly' (John 10.10) and 'The Life has
appeared; we saw it, we testify to it, we bring you word of
that eternal Life which . . . was disclosed to us' (I John
1.2, Moffatt). The all-important truths about ETERNAL LIFE
are that it is a *quality* of life, that it is first and foremost
the life of God, and that, as his gift in his Son, it is also the
life of man (believing in the Son) in the age-to-come now
inaugurated.

and this life is in his Son

Read 'and that this life. . . .' This clause is not an
added, independent statement about 'the life'. The testimony is in two parts: (*a*) that God has given eternal life
to men, and (*b*) that his Son mediates the gift.

12. He that hath the Son hath life: and he that hath not the Son of God hath not life

The inescapable logic of Christian theology, in Johannine
terms. The Greek order emphasises HATH in 12a: that is,
the man who possesses the Son *has actual possession* of
(eternal) life. It emphasises LIFE in 12b: that is, whatever
else the 'Sonless' man has, he does not have *life*. That is
beyond his grasp. Already (in e.g. 1.3 and 2.23) John has
insisted on the vital place of the SON—belief in the Son,
fellowship with the Son—in any true Christianity. The
heretics disagreed. Here they are told bluntly that by this
folly they forfeit eternal life.

THE CERTAINTIES OF TRUE BELIEF

5.13-20

(1) *You know you have eternal life* (v. 13)

'This letter is to assure you that you have eternal life.

It is addressed to those who give their allegiance to the Son of God' (NEB). We take THESE THINGS to be more probably not 'this letter' *in toto* but the passage 5.1-12. (Parallelism with John's Gospel (20.31), though marked, should not compel the NEB translation.)

In this verse John does not actually say 'you know you have eternal life'; simply that he has been writing to them in this manner THAT they MAY KNOW that, believing, as they do, in the Son, they HAVE ETERNAL LIFE. The verse, then, looks back to the previous section; 'The Blessings of True Belief'. The use in v. 13, however, of the verb *oida*, KNOW, which recurs five times in the remaining eight verses (and gives them their distinctive character) seems to us to bind v. 13 also to vv. 14-20, 'The Certainties of True Belief'. Their assurance (which John has now given them) that in the Son they possess eternal life is indeed the comprehensive certainty which assures to them those which follow.

And that ye may believe on the name of the Son of God
These words in AV should be omitted.

13, 15, 18-20. Ye may know that. . . . We know that
The YE, of course, as throughout the Epistle (see on 1.1-3a), is not opposed to WE. Here 'you', the Church, is addressed by 'me' (the 'I' of *egrapsa*), also the Church. YE becomes WE when, in the finale of the letter, John affirms on behalf of readers, himself, and the whole Church: WE KNOW. The phrase WE KNOW THAT (*oidamen hoti*), frequent in the New Testament, 'introduces a well-known fact that is generally accepted.'[1]

(2) *You know your worthy prayers are granted* (vv. 14-17).

---

[1] Bauer, *A Greek-English Lexicon of the New Testament*, tr. Arndt and Gingrich, p. 558.

14. And this is the confidence. . . .

The Christian enjoys fearless freedom in prayer in his Father's presence. The matter of 3.21 f., (see above) is now developed. In prayer, whenever we rightly ask, God listens to us. *Christians'* prayer, of course, is under discussion. Confidence that God listens to us springs from our family relationship with him, our Father. No earthly father (worth the name) is deaf to his children's petitions; no more is God. Even so, there is a limit to his hearing and our asking. Our right asking, we learned in 3.21 f., implies our obedience to God.[1] Now, we learn, God hears us in whatever we ask ACCORDING TO HIS WILL. Dodd points us aptly to the Lord's Prayer ('Thy kingdom come: thy will be done') and his prayer in Gethsemane ('Not as I will, but as thou wilt . . . thy will be done', Matt. 26.39, 42) as giving the very essence of right prayer, of asking which God does hear. Fundamentally, as someone has said, 'prayer is not a crying up the chimney of the universe to a celestial Santa Claus'; it is an aligning of our wills with God's sovereign will.

15. When we know God hears what we ask aright, WE also KNOW THAT WE HAVE THE PETITIONS THAT WE DESIRED OF HIM. We know God not only hears but answers us. Moreover, he answers even while we ask. Note that John says, not 'we *shall* have', but WE HAVE our petitions. The Gospel warrant for this startling tense and truth is Mark 11.24: 'Whatever you pray for and ask, *believe you have got it,* and you shall have it' (Moffatt). 'Here is the paradox that contains the secret of prayer: that in proportion as it becomes real prayer it carries its answer within it.'[2]

16a. These words apply this prayer-principle to intercession

[1] Cp. John 15.7, where it involves our abiding in Christ, and John 14.14, our prayer 'in the name of Christ'.

[2] Dodd, p. 135.

for a sinning BROTHER. (John does not consider the issue of intercession for the non-Christian. Cp. John 17.9.) This man is guilty of (what we might dare to call) 'ordinary' sin: A SIN WHICH IS NOT UNTO DEATH.

Not that John takes any misdemeanour lightly! ALL UN-RIGHTEOUSNESS IS SIN (v. 17). But he does recognise (vv. 16a, 17b) that even a sincere Christian brother—overborne by momentary folly, carelessness, human weakness—may sin, that God has provided a means for his forgiveness (cp. 1.7–2.2), and that it belongs to Christian fellowship to petition God on his behalf. God's will to restore this man is known: prayer to this end accords with God's will. All the strength of certainty that such prayer is heard and granted (vv. 14 f.) applies to this case. 'He will ask, and God will give him life' (RSV).

he shall ask, and he shall give him (*autō*, dative) life for them (dative) that sin not unto death

This is a literal translation of rather puzzling Greek. (a) Who HE is—the second 'he'—is debatable. Grammar favours HE being in both cases the same, the interceding brother. Brooke says: 'In virtue of his intercession . . . the Christian may be said to "give" life.' Cp. James 5.15, 20. The alternative is intrinsically more probable. Understand 'God' as the second HE, the subject of SHALL GIVE. So RSV and NEB.

(b) The AV obscures the fact that HIM (the sinning brother) and FOR THEM are in the same case, and are the same people. The change of number is as awkward in Greek as English. Moffatt compromises with: 'for him—for anyone who does not commit a deadly sin'.

There is a sin unto death: I do not say that he shall pray for it

Here not the Greek but the idea is puzzling. What is A SIN UNTO DEATH? (1) It is so serious that John, who knows

God's wide forgiveness, doubts if prayer for such a sin can
be right. (He does not forbid it but cannot commend it.)
(2) Its essence appears to be deliberate wilful defiance:
witting subversion of God's known purpose and truth; sin
'with a high hand and a haughty heart'.[1] Such sin was
known to Rabbinic Judaism and the Church later as 'mortal' and unforgivable—contrasted with forgivable sins of
ignorance, impulse and passion: 'venial' sins. (So here
the contrast with SIN NOT UNTO DEATH.) Similar to the SIN
UNTO DEATH in character, and similarly beyond forgiveness, is the sin against the Holy Ghost (Mark 3.29) and
apostasy of once baptised Christians (Heb. 6.4-6). (3) The
form here in mind is probably apostasy, with special
reference to denial of the Incarnate Christ by former
believers.

John could defend his attitude by Mark 8.38, or Luke
12.9; 'He that denieth me before men shall be denied before the angels of God', or some parallel tradition known
to him. But Dodd wisely writes: 'It was not for nothing
that the Church which preserved . . . the severe saying of
the Lord about the sin of denying Him, also preserved the
story of Peter's denial, of Christ's prayer for him, and of
his ultimate recovery (Mark 14.66-72; Luke 22.31-34; John
21.15-17)'.[2]

John's questioning of the apostate's right to the Church's
intercessions is wrung out of him, we suspect, by the
anguish to himself and peril to the Church just such sinners
were causing. The Church as a whole since has believed his
judgment harsh and wrong. If, however, its origin is severe
emotional stress rather than coldly misguided theological
reflection, we may find John's fault the more 'venial'. In
any event, we should not exaggerate the importance of v.
16b. It appears in John's argument merely as a rare exception to be fleetingly noted.

[1] Barclay, p. 138.
[2] Dodd, p. 137.

17. 'Although all wrong-doing is sin, not all sin is deadly sin' (NEB). This non-mortal—'normal'—sin, serious yet forgivable, is John's main concern in vv. 14-17.

(3) You know you are kept safe from sin's enslavement (v. 18)

We know that whosoever is born of God (*gegennēmenos*) sinneth not

The Christian (WHOSOEVER IS BORN OF GOD), born into the family of God, SINNETH NOT, i.e. does not habitually sin, does not live in sin. (See on 3.6 f.)

but he that is begotten of God keepeth himself

The AV is misled and misleading. The better Greek text, more accurately translated, is: 'but he who *was* born (*gennētheis*: in contrast to *gegennēmenos* above) of God keeps *him*'. The likeliest meaning then is: Christ keeps the Christian. Cp. John 17.12, 15. John's writings yield no exact parallel for BEGOTTEN OF GOD applied to Christ, but note the variant reading at John 1.13.

and that wicked one toucheth him not

Moffat: 'and the evil one never catches him', i.e. to enslave him. 'The Christian has an active enemy, but he has also a watchful guardian.'[1]

This third great certainty Christians have. In the family of God, Christ the eldest Brother of all God's children is there to preserve them against the recurrent assaults of the Wicked One. This, says John, WE KNOW: it is our common knowledge and experience. John, who has been quite open about the Christian's frequent lapses, must mean here: 'Thanks to the "watchful Guardian", the Christian—even

[1] B. F. Westcott, quoted by Barclay, pp. 142 f.

I

if he falls at times—never can become a helpless, unresisting
slave to sin's power. He is kept by the power of the Un-
defeatable.'

(4) *You know your standing—and where the world stands*
    (v. 19)

At the last, as earlier, John presses home the radicality
of the Christian-pagan division. WE KNOW THAT WE ARE OF
GOD AND (sc. that) THE WHOLE WORLD LIETH IN WICKEDNESS
(better, ' in the power of the evil one '). This is our Christian reading of the realities of earthly existence. On the one
hand, ourselves, ' of God ', passed from death unto life
(3.14); on the other, the whole set-up of pagan society,
driven by the devil and dwelling in death (cp. 2.15-17;
3.8-15). The antithesis is unqualified: the option literally
life or death. The challenge implicit here is tremendous.
Compromise with paganism compromises our ' life '; we toy
with ' death '. However tempting, yielding is unthinkable
for us, for WE KNOW our ' place ' and the world's.

But, the verse, challenging though its content is, stands
primarily as a great reassuring certainty. The main weight
of WE KNOW falls on THAT WE ARE OF GOD. From 3.1 on-
wards John's effort has been sustained to convince his faithful to shed every doubt of their ' being of God '. He would
have good reason to believe that by now, as a result, his
readers are ready to exult with him in saying—all trace of
question mark departed—WE KNOW THAT WE ARE OF GOD.

Moreover, the force of the certainty of v. 18 may be
meant to bear on v. 19 thus. We know the pagan world is
oppressively powerful and that to resist its pressures is not
only vital but desperately difficult. Yet we do not despair.
Why? Because we are sure that we belong to God and, as
such, that the whole power of God is exerted for our
defence (Dodd). Christ—who has overcome the world—
keeps us: with him, we meet even the challenge of the

dead and death-dealing ' world ' with confidence of triumph, and of ' life ' kept inviolate to the last.

(5) *You know you know the true God* (v. 20)

The very essence of true belief is that it should be belief in the true! The crowning certainty John shares with his readers is precisely this: that their sure faith in the Incarnation has enabled them to know HIM THAT IS TRUE, and that with him, THE TRUE GOD, they are in union, through Christ.

Three times in this penultimate verse of the letter comes the word TRUE (*alēthinos*).[1]

Dodd (like Moffatt) translates TRUE as ' real ' and paraphrases HIM THAT IS TRUE as ' Him who is the final reality '. The Christian, that is, knows himself brought into knowledge of, and communion with, Ultimate Reality. In this he achieves the goal which the Greek (Plato-influenced) world of the first century also set itself.

Yet in two points John's TRUE and TRUTH must be understood to depart from anything to which a non-Christian Hellenist could have subscribed. (1) HIM THAT IS TRUE, THE TRUE GOD is fully personal in meaning for John. (For a Hellenist, God was merely a convenient name for abstract Being.) Christians, who KNOW HIM THAT IS TRUE, know Ultimate Reality as a Divine Person, with whom they have Person-to-person relationship and communion. (2) Christian knowledge of Ultimate Reality explicitly depends on revelation of it *in history*. ' We know that the Son of God has come, and has given us understanding, to know him who is true ' (RSV). Ultimate reality has been manifested and ' beheld ' (John 1.14) on the plane of history, and thereby we know it. An idea which would mystify and repel the

[1] On ' truth ', see also commentary at 1.6; 2.19-21; 3.18 f.; and ' Life implies Truth ', 3.19–4.6; on ' true ' at 2.8.

non-Christian Hellenist religionist! To him all that is in
the world we see, touch and handle, all that comes and
passes away, the material and fleshly and 'phenomenal', is
illusory. All historical event is '*un*real'. It can tell us
nothing, indeed can only mislead us, about the Real.

Provided we remember these noted points of radical
divergence from Hellenism, we may not be misled if we
follow Dodd in interpreting TRUE in this 'Greek' way—as
'real'. But we have our doubts. Dodd's way treats *alēthinos*
(true or real) as if it and its cognate *alētheia* (truth) had no
history of usage outside the Greek pagan world. In fact they
had also a history in the LXX. In it, we recall,[1] *alētheia*
regularly translates the Hebrew *emeth*, the root-meaning of
which is reliability, faithfulness: primarily in God, then in
man. Similarly in e.g. (LXX) Ex. 34.6; Num. 14.18, *alēthinos* is used of God, meaning 'true', in the sense of
'dependable'; in Isa. 65.16, of God in contrast to other
gods who are not 'genuine'. Out of numerous biblical
examples listed by Bauer[2], the only clear instances of *alēthinos* in the Greek Platonist sense of 'real' (i.e. opposed
to 'illusory') are Heb. 8.2; 9.24; Luke 16.11. 'Reliable',
'dependable', 'genuine', are almost regularly the New
Testament meanings of *alēthinos*. Our v. 20 need be no
exception. We may still use the word 'real' in translation.
It will mean—on this interpretation—'genuine'; its oppo-
site not the unreal or illusory but the false, the counterfeit.

The Christian God is the real or genuine one in that he
is 'the One who alone completely corresponds to his
"Name"', who 'fulfils the highest conception of God-
head'.[3] He it is who is God indeed.[4] It is of this God (over

[1] See discussion at 1.6.

[2] *Op. cit.*, p. 36.

[3] Brooke, p. 151.

[4] Consider the term ' " true " or " real " friend '. The implied contrast
is not with an illusory or non-existent friend, but with one false to what
friendship means. A true friend embodies in his person and action all
that is most noble and profound in the concept ' friend '.

against all false conceptions of God otherwise had) that we
have been enabled to have knowledge, through Christ
come.

We are in him that is true, even in his Son Jesus Christ

Through Christ we are actually in union with no falsely
conceived approximation of God but with the real God.
We thus take the repeated HIM THAT IS TRUE in v. 20 to
refer both times to God. Some related it the first time to
God, the second time to Christ. Their case is twofold: (*a*)
that the phrase which AV translates EVEN IN HIS SON JESUS
CHRIST is in apposition to the second HIM THAT IS TRUE; and
(*b*) that John, like Paul, regularly speaks of our being in
union with *Christ*, not with God. But we find the change of
personal reference in HIM THAT IS TRUE awkward and unlikely. John means: 'We have union with the true God,
through his Son Jesus Christ', i.e. in virtue of our relationship with him and his with the Father.

This is the true God

In strict Greek, THIS (*houtos*) should refer to the last
person named. This would give, here: 'This Person,
namely Jesus Christ, is the true God.' More probably, in
accordance with a recognised Johannine literary mannerism
(cp. John 1.33; I John 2.22), THIS refers 'to the previous
subject as previously described'.[1] The meaning then is:
'God as just described—as made truly known in Jesus
Christ—is the true God.'

But Dodd—we think rightly—goes further still. Some
sweepingly comprehensive utterance seems demanded to
round off John's 'Christian certainties', and his letter, in
worthy manner. Picture John mentally gathering up ' all that '

[1] Brooke, p. 152.

(throughout the letter) 'he has been saying about God—
how He is light, and love, how He is revealed as the Father
through His Son Jesus Christ; how He is faithful and just
to forgive our sins; how He remains in us'.[1] All THIS, he
declares, IS THE TRUE GOD! Seen thus, THIS fills with great
richness the last of John's certainties. 'You know you know
the true God; *such* a God!'

And eternal life

Grammatically ETERNAL LIFE is in strict apposition to
THE TRUE GOD. Nowhere, however, is God called LIFE—
Christ is life (John 11.25; 14.6)—although John 5.26, 'the
Father hath life in himself', comes very close to it. It seems
best to follow Moffatt: 'This is the real God, this is life
eternal', which Dodd expounds as 'This is the Real God
and knowledge of Him is eternal life.' Cp. John 17.3: 'This
is life eternal, that they might know thee the only true
God.'

THE FINAL WARNING:
BEWARE ALL COUNTERFEITS

5.21

Little children, keep yourselves from idols

The word *eidōla* (IDOLS) curiously epitomises the factors
involved in interpreting 'truth' and 'true'. In pagan Greek,
eidōla was Plato's technical word for the 'unreal' (as he
saw them) objects of sense-experience, in contrast to the
'ideal' real; in LXX, *eidōla* translated the Hebrew 'false
gods', i.e. counterfeit deities, over against the one genuine
God. The latter is its Christian meaning.[2]

---

[1] Dodd, p. 140.
[2] This makes us all the more chary of taking *alēthinos* in any but its
LXX sense of 'genuine'.

What are the IDOLS here? Barclay[1] considers that John (knowing his readers and knowing the outstanding idolatry of pagan Ephesus, notably connected with the Temple of Diana) means simply and directly: 'Keep yourselves from the pollutions of heathen worship.' Contamination by contact with these pagan practices must have been extremely difficult for an Ephesian Christian to avoid. Yet they had to be avoided, or blasphemous nonsense was made of all these great certainties—above all of WE . . . KNOW HIM THAT IS TRUE. It could be in John's psychology[2] to make his noble proclamations of vv. 13-20, esp. vv. 18-20, and then bring their total purport abruptly to bear, at the very last, upon a burning practical issue facing his readers. 'You who know you know the truth and the true God: *do* the truth! Keep away from all places and objects of heathen worship.'

Attractive. It is, however, inherently likelier that in the very last sentence the focus is kept broad. In its position, v. 21 must surely be a 'big' verse. If *specific* idols are in John's mind they must be genuinely serious rivals[3] to the true God in claiming the readers' belief. Such were the false gods of the heretics' construction. These had great appeal and their devotees great power. A substantial purpose of John throughout the letter had been to expose them and warn his readers of the extremely grave threat these idols constituted. It is natural, and no 'come-down', if now, with the last strokes of his pen, John is rousing his readers, girt with the certainty that they have the one genuine God and the strength that certainty brings, to beware contamination by the bogus 'gods' whose worship the Cerinthian seceders propagated. Their deceitfulness, unresisted, could deal death to the readers' life.

But do the vulgar idols of the Temple of Diana and the

[1] *Op. cit.*, pp. 144-146.
[2] Cp. in this, 3.16-18.
[3] As, for example, Diana and her like could hardly be.

intellectually respectable idols of the anti-Christian Asian seceders—even when taken together—exhaust the content of the IDOLS from which the LITTLE CHILDREN are to KEEP themselves? No. In its context we see v. 21 as the most sweeping possible injunction:

> ' You know you know the true God. You are in communion with him. Him you know, defined in Jesus Christ his Son who came, and in the several ways which this letter has set forth. And from him comes your eternal life. Then guard yourselves against accommodation to belief in, and practice of, anything other than that which is completely genuine and true, anything in less than full accord with worship of our true God.'

In these last words, they are tersely told that they must apply their surely-possessed knowledge of the genuine as the touchstone of all else, and reject and abstain from all that the touchstone rejects.

In our days, State-worship, sub- and quasi-Christian religious cults and resurgent non-Christian religions (which in some cases, in their modern dress, have assimilated much of Christianity), are to be seen as the ' idols ' they are and ' kept from '.

Nineteen centuries after John we recognise, better than he could, a Christian obligation—with genuine Christian love for the benighted as well as the enlightened, and with a strong missionary kind of tolerance—to associate with the ' half-lights ', even the ' false lights '. But his word still applies: ' Be on your guard. There is but one God who is God indeed. For him, whom you know in the Son of God who came, there is no substitute whatever. To your true God, wherever you be placed, however you be tempted by any idol, stay adamantly true. For " He is the true God— and eternal life ".'

THE SECOND & THIRD EPISTLES
OF JOHN

INTRODUCTION

These little letters need but little introduction.

Who wrote them? Most probably the author of I John (and the Fourth Gospel): John the Elder. This has been sometimes disputed. (See Dodd or Brooke for full discussion.) For example, (*a*) why was I John early canonised and called 'of John', yet universal acceptance of II and III John was long delayed? (*b*) Why, in some Church centres where I and II John were accepted, was there silence on III John? And (*c*) why, in other centres where all three were known, were two authors held responsible, one for I John, one for II and III John? We would answer (*a*) and (*b*) thus, that silence on III John, and indeed on both tiny Epistles, so brief and so lacking in quotable matter, is insignificant and easily understood. We can appreciate, too, how (*c*) arose. The close structural similarity of II and III John, together with the same internal attribution (II John 1; III John 1) to 'the Elder', labels them one man's work. Yes: but can he really have written I John also? To many critics, II John has appeared such a 're-hash' of I John that they conclude that II John could never have been by the author of I John himself, and that it is a fabrication, consciously imitative of I John, by 'the Elder' who wrote both later Epistles. We believe their conclusion mistaken. Who would have bothered to invent II John? Who could have 'imitated' I John in II John quite so cleverly, achieving such linguistic closeness to I John in the main, and yet just sufficient independence as to warrant II John being taken for an original composition? Common authorship—that of 'the Elder', John of

Ephesus—for all three Epistles has least to oppose it and most to commend it.

Who received them? We found I John to be written by the Elder to his Asian diocese. II John also is a pastoral letter, but written to a single church in that diocese. III John, a genuinely private letter, addresses a single individual in an Asian church. See notes on II John 1 (The Lady) and III John 1.

Why was II John written? (For fuller answer see the commentary.)

II John is written to a church whose members need to be alerted to the existence of impostors and antichrists who 'have emerged in the world, men who will not acknowledge the coming of Jesus Christ in the flesh' (Moffatt, II John 7); 'advanced' Christians who 'will not remain by the doctrine of Christ' (*ibid.* v. 9). The Elder exhorts them to love one another (v. 5) (as in I John), to 'watch themselves' (v. 8) and not even to speak to these heretics if they should come to that congregation (v. 10). The similarity to the situation dealt with in I John is evident. But whereas I John's readers seem already embroiled in conflict with the heretics, II John's church appears to have been so far without first-hand experience of the seceding heretics. Is II John, then, a prelude to I John? Does it reflect an early stage in the heretical trouble which, when it later spread and raged at its fiercest, occasioned I John at a diocesan level? This seems a reasonable view until we observe that, all in all, II John is better described as a 'cut-down' I John than is I John as a 'blown-up' II John. By itself, II John would be rather enigmatic. Phrases such as 'in the truth' (vv. 1, 4), 'in truth and love' (v. 3), 'deceiver' and 'antichrist' (v. 7), 'advanced' (*proagōn*, v. 9), almost 'need for their understanding the fuller exposition given in the longer writing' (Dodd). We conclude that I John came first addressed to a wide area. Then II John was sent, perhaps only a little later, to a particular church in the area which the Elder

knew to be about to face, for the first time, the trial of
having the heretics, already active in most of the diocese
(hence the earlier need of I John), doing their upsetting
work in its midst.

The relation between I and II John is not unlike that
observed between an American Presidential candidate's
nation-wide TV 'set' speech and any of his 'whistle-stop'
five-minute addresses given on campaign tour. Nine-tenths
of the substance of the latter is from the big speech, greatly
cut down in volume. It uses the language and recalls and
presupposes knowledge of the main speech. It has some
additional emphasis on the local situation and some 'snap'
practical advice for local party action.

In the light of this last sentence we perhaps best understand vv. 10 f., the only substance in II John not in I John:
crude, sharp, even harsh, words of practical injunction to
boycott the heretics. These are words called forth by the
urgent local need; words which in the more studied, gener-
alised, earlier Epistle the Elder stopped short of writing.

Why was III John written? In its concern III John stands
quite apart from the other two. Its issue is authority, not
doctrine. In one congregation under the charge of the Elder
a man called Diotrephes has been proving difficult. Itinerant
missionaries sent (probably) from John's own church and
with his authority and blessing have not been received in
that congregation, despite the willingness of some of its
members to welcome them. Diotrephes, with those members he has won to his side, has been responsible. And not
only has he banned the missionaries but driven out of the
local church its members who opposed him and his ban.
John tells us (v. 9) that he has written a letter to the church.
He must have doubted, however, that it would get safely—
past Diotrephes—to an unbiased reading by the members.
So John also writes to a trusty friend, Gaius, a member
either of that church or a neighbouring one. This letter is
our III John. He writes to commend Gaius for his loyalty

and kindness to the travelling evangelists, to expose Diotrephes 'as an ambitious demagogue with a turn for vitu-
perative rhetoric' (Dodd, p. lviii) directed against John,
and as a man who has arrogated to himself power to turn
away the Elder's missionaries and expel their supporters
from the church. And he writes to confirm Gaius in his
imitation not of evil (viz. Diotrephes' high-handed conduct)
but good (v. 11). Demetrius, warmly commended (v. 12),
may have been leader of the missionaries or bearer of this
letter to Gaius: maybe both.

Every commentator confesses to irritation that into such
an interesting situation in late first-century church life the
Elder has given us no more than a glimpse. But it is enough
to reveal a stage—after the apostles' death and when the
Elders, their 'disciples', were aged—during which the local
congregations in Asia were restive under the Elders' leader-
ship, so old (and so old-fashioned?) and so distant.[1] The
plaint from the churches may have been: 'Why should we
not settle our own affairs for ourselves within our own congregation? Why should these itinerant evangelists, with the
Elder's commission, be given automatic *entrée* into our
church fellowship and community, and be allowed to upset,
as likely as not, much good work we have been quietly
doing?' Diotrephes' action may have been in answer to
this acute sense of frustration in the local situation, created
by the Elder's remote but powerful control.

This is to put the best complexion on the conduct of
Diotrephes. John saw it as plain flouting of his authority
and wrote III John as part of his corrective campaign. The
preservation of the letter suggests that he succeeded in
'putting in his place' Diotrephes 'who loveth to have the
pre-eminence among them' (v. 9). Time, however, favoured
not the Elder but local strong men, lay or clerical, and led

---

[1] Each church had its local presbyters, of course, but real authority still
rested, it seems, with the Elder in whose 'diocese' some particular Asian
church lay.

to the establishment, in the course of the second century, of the local episcopate.

III John is a valued glimpse of the tension in the Church in Asia shortly preceding that resolution of the question of authority.

Date: about the same time as I and II John—say, AD 96.

II JOHN

1-3

Comparison and contrast of vv. 1-3 with III John 1-2 is instructive. Papyrus letters of this time show that the greeting of III John (its distinctively Christian touches apart) is precisely that of a contemporary private letter. The salutation of II John has, overall, a similar cast. But it is so much more theologically overlaid and so ponderous that at once we doubt whether such a greeting can really be intended to preface a private letter and address one particular individual. (Doubt amply confirmed by study of 'the Lady', v. 1. See below.)

Another feature of the epistolary introduction comes to light in v. 3. At this point the greeting proper would be expected. Its usual secular form would be simply 'Greetings! (Acts 15.23; James 1.1)'. The usual New Testament form would be 'Grace be to you and peace. . . . ! (Gal. 1.3)' or 'Grace, mercy and peace (be to you). . . . ! (I Tim. 1.2; II Tim. 1.2)'. In II John 3, however, we find expressed not a wish, not strictly a greeting at all, but an assurance. The Greek reads (as in RSV): 'Grace, mercy and peace will be (*estai*) with us. . . .' The Elder's greeting is thus not pious prayer but promise of sure blessings. (Cp. I Peter 5.10, in AV and RSV.)

1. *The Elder*

Cp. III John 1. The word *presbyteros* means (1) an elderly man; (2) (in the Jewish and Christian Church) an elder, i.e. one who with fellow-elders taught and governed in some single local congregation; and (3) (for a brief period in the province of Asia, and perhaps there alone) one of 'the Elders', a group, seemingly small, of Christian leaders who had been 'disciples of the apostles' (Irenaeus, *Adv. Haer.* V 36) and therefore formed the direct link between the eye-witnesses of Jesus' ministry and the Church of the late first century.

The writer's authoritative tone in the letters suggests that the term THE ELDER carries more than the weight of his age. At best, sense (1) above is inadequate here. Is the author then an elder in sense (2)? No. His authority was not limited to any single congregation but exercised over several. And it was authority which, if sometimes locally and temporarily usurped (as in III John), was within his group of churches—his diocese, almost—quite *unshared*. The author is, most likely, one of the Elders as defined in (3). Irenaeus, himself from Asia, actually refers several times to the Elder. No name is mentioned. Such prestige did this man enjoy that the title alone sufficiently identified him for the whole community of Christians Irenaeus addressed. Papias, also from Asia, speaks, too, simply of 'the Elder'. He may or may not be the same man as Irenaeus' Elder. In Papias' case the Elder appears from the context to be called John. This John we have taken to be THE ELDER of II and III John and the author of all three Johannine Epistles.

The Lady

unto the elect lady and her children

Our suspicion above that II John is no ordinary private letter to an individual is deepened by this mode of address. (Cp. v. 5, and v. 13, 'the children of thy elect sister', for the same rather precious speech.)

The Greek, of course, would admit of a quite matter-of-

K

fact rendering. THE ELECT LADY, *eklektē kyria*, could signify a real named person, 'the lady Electa' or 'the elect Kyria'. Either Electa or Kyria (or both) could be proper names. Clement of Alexandria is alleged to have held that II John was written 'to a Babylonian woman named Electa who signifies the Catholic Church'. Rendel Harris understood the phrase as 'my dear Electa' and thought she was a Gentile proselyte of the tribe of Ruth and, like her, a widow! Verse 13, however, seems to be a death-blow to Electa: it is too strange for credence that her sister should have the same name. What about 'the elect Kyria'? Kyria is a well-attested proper name, meaning 'mistress', corresponding to the name Martha in Aramaic and Dom(i)na in Latin. *Eklektē* as an epithet (meaning 'eminent') attached to a proper name is also established (cp. Rom. 16.13, RSV). Certainly 'the elect Kyria' is more defensible, as a genuine individual person, than 'the lady Electa'. But is she probable? The letter speaks of the recipient's children—some with her, some not; some good Christians, some not—and of a sister and her children living beside the writer. It tells of how the recipient is loved by not only the Elder but all true Christians everywhere. The letter shows passionate interest in this large family circle, and yet neither sister nor child nor nephew nor niece is named.[1] Extraordinary! Further, despite such intimate 'familiar' interest, the letter treats no domestic issues. So, we may dismiss the idea of 'eminent Kyria' or any other proper name! This is a pastoral, not a private, letter.

THE ELECT LADY AND HER CHILDREN must stand for a local church and its members. (Not the whole catholic Church, since (as Dodd remarks) it has no 'sister'.) The 'sister' (v. 13) will be another local congregation in, like the elect lady, the Asian diocese. Female personification of a community was common enough. Israel, for example, was

[1] Contrast III John which, brief as it is, presents vividly, as named individuals, Gaius, Diotrephes and Demetrius.

'daughter of Zion' We still speak of Britannia; the French, of Marianne. In the instance before us personification may simply be a literary conceit. It may, however, be a deliberate safety device, in case the letter reached hostile hands. Persecution, such as compelled Revelation's prudent use of symbolic names and imagery, may not have been far off in Asia.

The word ELECT, here and in v. 13, will now have its theological sense, of 'chosen', 'called'. (Cp. I Peter 5.13: 'She in Babylon called together with you', i.e. your sister-church in Rome.)

1-3. *The Truth*

Four times in these three verses John uses the word TRUTH. Already his mind may be upon the contrasting 'lie' against which in vv. 7-9 he has to warn. But more than that. Through the term TRUTH he is able to express, from the outset, the depth of his love for, and solidarity with, the readers—and not only his own but that of the whole Christian fellowship (v. 1)—and express, too, the *ground* of their loving concern (vv. 1-2); and it is by the linking again of TRUTH and LOVE in v. 3 that he moves skilfully into the theme of the NEW COMMANDMENT, in vv. 4-6.

1. whom I love in the truth

Not just 'truly', or 'sincerely', but 'with a love "which corresponds to the truest conception of love"'' (Brooke, p. 170). The background-thought is e.g. I John 3.19; 5.20; and 3.16; 4.10-11. Since, as Christians, we are of the truth, we know and exercise true love, love that is love indeed: WE LOVE IN THE TRUTH.

Possibly something further is intended. Truth is the sphere in which Christians live, act and are related. Then, WHOM I LOVE IN THE TRUTH may mean 'whom in virtue of our common bond (our common Christian knowledge of the true God, membership of the true fellowship and obliga-

tions of true conduct) I love'. In this case, the Elder pro-
fesses here, as in III John 1, not, or not only, the quality of
his love for the church addressed. He is establishing at
once his solidarity with them, viz. the common *locus* 'in
the truth' which he and they have.

also all they that have known the truth
Christian believers everywhere.

2. For the truth's sake
Passionate fidelity to the truth revealed in Christ is what
inspires the Elder and the whole Church to this obedient
love within the fellowship.

3. in truth and love
The closing words of the introduction. They may simply
define respectively the revelation of GOD THE FATHER and
the work of THE LORD JESUS CHRIST. But since (see above
on 'The Greeting') v. 3 is no wish but a statement of what
'will be' (*estai*), the phrase IN TRUTH AND LOVE gains the
force of a proviso. That is, GRACE . . . MERCY AND PEACE
will be our assured blessings, provided our Christianity
shows the necessary marks of TRUTH AND LOVE, of true belief and loving practice. Cp. I John 3.23.

THE ENTREATY AND THE COMMANDMENT

4-6

4. I rejoiced greatly . . .
Cp. III John 3. The Elder follows normal epistolary cus-
tom in beginning his letter proper by expressing pleasure
at having had good news of those to whom he writes. Dodd
cites (p. 158) a letter (AD 70-80) beginning, 'Chaeremon to
his dearest Apollonius, greeting. I received your note. . . .
On reading it, I rejoiced that you were well, with all your
family. . . .'

I found

Probably through reports of travelling brethren such as III John 3 specifies.

of thy children walking in truth

OF here means 'some of . . .' Not all the elect lady's children, evidently, had been WALKING IN TRUTH, i.e. living a soundly, faithfully, Christian life. (On 'walking', see I John 1.6; on 'truth', II John 1-3.) The Church was divided.

as we have received a commandment from the Father

i.e. as we were comanded to do by the Father, to walk in truth and love (v. 3). Probably the command in the dual form of I John 3.23 (true belief and brotherly love) is in John's mind here and in the Epistle as a whole. Verse 5, however, does cite the commandment in its single (John 15.12) form: LOVE ONE ANOTHER.

5. This verse, the 'entreaty' of our heading, is notable for its graciousness. The Elder, mightily powerful man as he is, does not presume to command this local church. He begs (RSV), beseeches (AV) or entreats (Moffatt) it. The use again of the term LADY at this point adds to the gentle courtesy of his approach. But he is entirely firm in his purpose. He is grieved by the rift (implied in v. 4) in this church fellowship. Brotherly love, he knows, is the only cure. So his entreaty is in the form of a recall to THE COM-MANDMENT, NEW—yet old, and FROM THE BEGINNING, not his but Christ's, THAT WE LOVE ONE ANOTHER. Cp. I John 2.7 f., and notes.

6. And this is love, that we walk after his commandments

Cp. I John 5.3a.

This is the commandment, That . . . ye should walk in it.

IN IT is 'in love'. Love to God means obedience to his commands (v. 6a); obedience to his commands means love to one another (vv. 6a, 5b).

THE WARNING

7-11

The theme now changes from the church's internal troubles (hinted at in vv. 4-6) to an imminent grave threat it faces from outside. This latter is the main topic and immediate occasion of the Epistle.

The change of theme is abrupt, the transition being made by the one word FOR (Greek, *hoti* 'because'). To us, at least, it means little without amplification. Dr Barclay (*Letters of John*, p. 163) helps us so far by filling out *hoti* thus: 'There is all the more reason to speak like this because . . .' But what is the 'speaking like this' to which vv. 7-11 look back, which unites the theme of the two passages? Such phrases, surely, as YE SHOULD WALK and AS YE HAVE HEARD FROM THE BEGINNING, in v. 6. Like the church, the heretics about to be described had failed to walk as they had heard from the beginning, i.e. had failed to live in accordance with the original Gospel and commandment. The church's departure had been from LOVE; the heretics', from TRUTH—that Gospel truth which was, and was heard, FROM THE BEGINNING and which, together with love, comprises the dual commandment in I John 3.23.

We look now more closely at the heretics as the Elder delineates and castigates them and warns against the peril they present.

7. *The Antichrist*

The essence of the heresy is: denial THAT JESUS CHRIST IS COME IN THE FLESH (AV), or denial of 'the coming of Jesus Christ in the flesh' (RSV). AV ignores, and RSV cleverly disguises, a slight complication in the Greek text. The literal rendering is 'who do not confess that Jesus Christ is coming' (present tense) 'in the flesh'. Strictly this would

imply current belief, and heretical denial of the belief, that
Jesus Christ would come (i.e. in the Second Advent) IN THE
FLESH. Of this belief there is no clear trace elsewhere. With
Dodd (p. 149) 'we assume that our writer is not skilled in
the niceties of Greek idiom' and that, despite his 'is
coming', he refers to precisely the heresy described in I
John (e.g. in I John 4.2 f.) as denial 'that Jesus Christ has
come in the flesh' (perfect tense).

The best commentary on the heresy (vv. 7, 9) is I John
4.2 ff., of which this passage 'is almost certainly a reminiscence' (Brooke, p. 175), and I John 2.18 ff., especially vv.
22-24. See also our notes on these earlier passages and in
Introduction to I John, pp. 31 ff. above, esp. 34-37.

The men arraigned by John in both epistles denied the
reality of the Incarnation of Jesus Christ. They distinguished Jesus (the human) from Christ (the Divine Son of
God) and so dissolved the unity of his Person. As we have
seen earlier, they thus cut away the vital roots of the Christian Gospel, for if the eternal Christ, the Son of God, did
not really live in the human flesh of Jesus of Nazareth and
really suffer and die in him, then, even in knowing Jesus,
we are without sure knowledge of God; and even in the
death of Jesus we are still without a sufficient means of our
forgiveness. All is gone, all that makes Christian teaching
unique and makes it Gospel.

John tells us in v. 7 that many deceivers have gone out
into the world, men who do not confess the real Incarnation of Jesus Christ. THIS, i.e. the man guilty of this kind
of heresy, IS THE DECEIVER AND THE ANTICHRIST. The heretics are many and missionary; neither silent nor static with
their lie. This we infer from v. 10 which implies that they
moved about and disseminated their doctrine, from I John
2.27 which suggests that they communicated teaching and
from I John 4.1 which alludes to them as false PROPHETS.
Dodd takes II John 7a also as testimony to the heretics'
wide activity as (in their own eyes) Christian missionaries

and compares ARE ENTERED INTO THE WORLD with Mark
16.15, GO YE INTO ALL THE WORLD. We doubt if this is
John's meaning. Their 'going out' here is, rather, as in I
John 2.19, from the Church fellowship (and orthodoxy)
INTO THE WORLD, the home of all at variance with Christian
truth.

The world may find the heretics congenial and the local
church's members may, unless forewarned, be attracted by
them, but John has their true measure. They are DECEIVERS.
Indeed, their heresy is the hallmark, as they are the embodiment, of the DECEIVER and the ANTICHRIST (v. 7b). In no
possible stronger terms could John condemn them. (For
fuller discussion of the Docetic 'lie' and of the term 'antichrist', etc. see on I John 2.18 f.)

9. Together with v. 7 we take v. 9. In it John puts his finger
for us on the feature of the heretics' attitude which he be-
lieves to have led to their pernicious Christology and their
separation from God. WHOSOEVER TRANSGRESSETH, AND
ABIDETH NOT IN THE DOCTRINE OF CHRIST, HATH NOT GOD.
The key-phrase is WHOSOEVER TRANSGRESSETH. The Greek,
pas ho proagōn, means 'everyone who goes ahead',
or 'advances', or 'advances too far' (Barclay). The un-
usualness of the word suggests that the heretics may well
have used it, styling themselves the 'go-aheads', in the
sense of 'progressives', 'advanced Christian thinkers' or
the like. They must have believed that, for intelligent people
(like themselves) belonging to a cultured Gentile civilisa-
tion, and for the winning of that Gentile world, Christian
doctrine must 'advance' out of its naïve Palestinian mould
into a shape recognisable by, and acceptable to, the pagan
intelligentsia of the time.

Now the Fourth Gospel and First Epistle show that John
himself saw the need for development. Indeed, they demon-
strate brilliantly how it should be made. But the heretics
had advanced too far. (See Introduction to I John, pp. 34-

39 above.) Whereas John had scrupulously avoided any compromise of the original Gospel when he expressed and interpreted it in terms known to Hellenism, the heretics (in misguided enthusiasm rather than malice, perhaps) had recklessly assimilated Christian doctrine to pagan Gnostic ideas, as well as language. Their 'lie' considered in v. 7 exemplifies the inevitable consequence. In the name of Christian progress they had cut adrift from the original DOCTRINE OF CHRIST. They 'advanced' the Christian Gospel out of all recognition—as Christian and as Gospel. They thought themselves the cream of Christian theologians: they are, John says, in fact, impostors (v. 7); and they are men without God at all (v. 9)! Since they do not abide in the teaching of the Son (perhaps with special reference to the Son's Fourth Gospel teaching about himself), they cannot possibly 'know' or 'have' the Son, i.e. believe in, and have fellowship with him. Then they do not 'have God' the Father either. The heretics would probably reply (see on I John 2.23): 'We need no Son to have the Father', but the Elder is as emphatic here as in the earlier epistle that WHOSOEVER DENIETH THE SON, THE SAME HATH NOT THE FATHER.[1]

Verse 9 deals with a perennially live issue in Christian circles: the nature and degree of development proper to Christian doctrine. The Church, it may be said, is a living organism, and what lives must develop or die. We have a *living* Christ and a *living* Spirit given to lead us into all truth. To turn our back upon all development is to deny them and ' to condemn Christian theology to lasting sterility ' (Dodd, p. 150). John would agree. We must take care not to accuse him here, unjustly, of vetoing any ' advance '. (As remarked before, his own contribution to an enriching re-interpretation of the original Palestinian Gospel was pro-

---

[1] There is probably an anticipatory sideglance at this aspect of the II John heresy in the emphatic phrasing in II John 3, ' the Lord Jesus Christ, the Son of the Father '.

found, and, in the truest sense, 'advance'.) What John does insist is that no 'advance' is legitimate which does not remain faithful to, and rooted in, THE DOCTRINE OF CHRIST, or, as Jude 3 has it, THE FAITH ONCE DELIVERED TO THE SAINTS. This *un*faithful, *up*rooted kind of developed doctrine John attacks, surely rightly. We need to guard against it still, as much as against the 'sterility' of an unadventurous clinging to the old and original, in form as well as substance, in Christian doctrine.

It is perhaps not too severely to caricature them to say that our contemporary schools, of Biblical Theology and of (what we might call) Existentialist Philosophic Theology, reflect this issue. Both face some danger. The former is so determined to be biblical and loyal to the DOCTRINE OF CHRIST as to appear sometimes obscurantist, indifferent to the language and insights of non-biblical scholars (e.g. in science and philosophy) and suspicious of the Christian character of any belief or practice—or even terminology— not specifically dominical and apostolic. The latter is so anxious to conciliate non-Christian philosophers and, very laudably, to communicate Christianity in terms which man can understand and accept today, that the Gospel it propagates may seem so metamorphosed, indeed so emasculated, as, at times, to have parted company with THE DOCTRINE OF CHRIST.

There is a *via media*. Though hard to find and harder to keep, John found it in his day, and for us in ours has pointed the way. (Vincent Taylor's *Person of Christ in New Testament Teaching* has this rare, right balance.)

8. *The Reward*

Look to yourselves that we lose not . . . but that we receive a full reward

RSV translates a Greek text which secures better sense: 'Look to yourselves that you may not lose what you have worked for, but may win a full reward.' A warning that easy-going tolerance of the Christological lie of the deceiver

and the Antichrist could place the faithful church members
where the heretics are, without possession of God (v. 9).
Thus it could deprive them of all they had striven for in
the Christian life, e.g. a place as accepted children and
'reapers' of God in the day when 'he that reapeth receiveth
wages, and gathereth fruit unto life eternal' (John 4.36).
And mention in v. 7 of Antichrist *come* makes the point of
v. 8 one of pressing urgency. 'This is the last hour: don't
jeopardise your reward now, now of all times.' See on I
John 2.18 f.

10-11. *The Prohibition*

The only teaching in II John without parallel in I John.
Dodd's commentary (pp. 150-153) provides the classic
treatment of John's idea of how to treat heretics.

John says: 'If somebody comes to you (his indicative
mood in a conditional clause implying that there is little
" if " about it!) and doesn't bring teaching in accord with
the fundamental truths of the Gospel, never take him over
your threshold and never give him a greeting, for to greet
him is to share in his wicked work.' For this last phrase,
IS PARTAKER OF HIS EVIL DEEDS, cp. I Tim. 5.22. 'To share
in the deeds of others means to be equally responsible for
them.'[1]

Thus the Elder prohibits any hospitality to visiting heretical Christian teachers. (Without that hospitality their pernicious work would be largely stopped. See on III John 5 f.)
True Christians have not even to say 'Hullo' to their
heretical Christian(?) 'brethren' in passing. An absolute
boycott of the heretics is demanded.

These are rather notorious verses. They sound thoroughly
uncharitable. They suggest an exclusivism and spiritual
arrogance more typical of Gnosticism than healthy Christianity. What has happened to John's convictions that God
loved and loves the world (heretics included, presumably),

[1] Bauer, *op. cit.*, p. 439.

and that our love, made real in action (I John 3.18), is the
sine qua non of any Christian soundness in dealings with
our brother?

An apologist for John might, however, raise three points
worth pondering. (1) John is clearly giving an *ad hoc* ruling
for immediate local action, in a situation in which—it
seems from I John—the very *survival* of the Church was in
the balance. He is not enunciating a general principle of
behaviour towards anyone we happen to dislike or dis-
approve of, in general.

(2) The heresy calling for counter-action is one of ultimate gravity: deviationism not at the circumference of the
faith but at its dead-centre. No hour or two's friendly
chat can put Antichrist right. Far sterner measures are
necessary.

(3) The boycott of the heretics *need* not be inconsistent
with Christian love. This is so whether the love considered
is for (*a*) the faithful members of this local church, (*b*) the
pagans surrounding it, or (*c*) the heretics soon to assail it.
Take them in turn.

(*a*) *The faithful* (if typical of the Asian Church as a
whole, as depicted in I John) include many ' weaker brethren '. John may feel, on the one hand, that, if exposed to
personal encounter with the glib heretics, they are too
frail to withstand; on the other, that he must prohibit any
mixing with the heretics, even socially, if he is not to be
misunderstood by the weaker brethren as acquiescing
in the heresy. Love for the brethren cannot take such
risks.

(*b*) *The pagans*, too, in Pergamum, or Sardis, or Philadelphia, etc.—whichever it be—cannot be permitted to be
confused by even *appearance* of orthodox indifference to
heretics' heresies. The boycott, significantly, is an overt,
public sign of the true Church's rejection of paganism even

when in Christian guise. The pagan community must see
that the Church passionately cares for the purity of its
truth.

(c) *The heretics*. Perhaps only ' shock treatment ' (severe,
but administered in love, and seeking, as love must, the
heretics' own highest interests) can bring them to recognise
their mis-belief as Antichrist. Forced to reflect on the ground
of their being ' sent to Coventry ', the Elder hopes, they will
see their sin in its heinousness, repent, and in due time be
restored to fellowship. So regarded, the boycott is a necessary phase in John's programme of 'redeeming' love for
the apostate. We might compare, in some measure, Paul's
policy in I Cor. 5.1-5 and its happy outcome in II Cor.
2.6-8.

These points at least temper our judgment of John. But
for many of us the question will remain: Is John's coun-
selled way of boycott *ever* the Christian way with heretics?
In a situation of such extreme peril for Christianity as the
Asian Christians may have faced, we ourselves might say
' Yes '. Without that experience we cannot give a dogmatic
' No '. Yet, with Dodd, we are bound to ' doubt whether this
(boycott) policy in the end best serves the cause of truth
and love. . . . Does truth prevail the more if we are not on
speaking terms with those whose view of the truth differs
from ours—however disastrous their error may be? ' (pp.
151-152). As for love, only by great straining (e.g. in 3(c)
above) can boycott ever be interpreted as love, not lovelessness. While firmness belongs to love, harshness does not,
and a policy solely consisting of severance of relations is
cold and negative and uncaring. It simply abandons the
erring ones to their error and doom. The demand of love, it
seems to us, involves continued caring, and caring calls for
continued personal relations.

John's verses, however, serve well to remind us that association with fundamentally perverted and perverting Christians, even if (on our understanding) obligatory, is also perilous. *Uncritical* association with such stands condemned. The tolerance on which we pride ourselves may symptomise not our strong love for our benighted brethren but indifference to truth—indifference all too soon revealed by our betrayal of it, in such company. In this event, we ourselves are lost, and the 'liars' are simply confirmed in their lie, and not—in any worthy sense of 'love'—loved at all!

The Christian summons, as we hear it, is to find, and hold steadfastly, the exacting middle way which combines devotion to truth and devotion to love. Devotion to love insists that we maintain caring personal contact even with those whose convictions are anathema to us; devotion to truth, that, in that contact, we abide, unswervingly, in the doctrine of Christ. We should perhaps stress that this desperately hard 'unswerving abiding' is vital not only for the truth's sake but for *love's* sake. We do not 'love' a heretic if we tacitly condone his lie, still less if, surrendering truth, we join him in his lie. In this context it is love's special function to present to the man the truth in us, in its purity.

How is this twofold fidelity to be maintained? Does not John tell us—elsewhere—better than anyone? 'Whatsoever is born of God overcometh the world' (I John. 5.4a); 'we know that anyone born of God does not sin, but he who was born of God (i.e. Christ) keeps him, and the evil one does not touch him' (I John 5.18, RSV); 'he who is in you is greater than he who is in the world' (I John 4.4, RSV). Even so it is not easy. 'Love is always relevant but never a simple possibility,'[1] and truth is always under threat by others' lies and our own specious love.

[1] R. Niebuhr, quoted by A. M. Hunter, *Introducing the New Testament*, SCM Press, 1945, p. 180.

THE CONCLUSION

12-13

12. ' I have much to write to you, but I do not care to put it down in black and white' (NEB). John plans to visit the church addressed. Then, no doubt, he will take up the MANY THINGS of v. 12 and develop the theme of vv. 7-11.

paper and ink
Papyrus and the rude ink (cp. III John 13; II Cor. 3.3) compounded of lamp-black and gum.

that our joy may be full
Cp. I John 1.4 (see notes); John 15.11. More than the natural joy of personal reunion: rather that of the whole Church made fully secure in its hold on truth and love, as the outcome of the letter and the Elder's visit.

13. The children of thine elect sister
i.e. 'the members of your sister-congregation', in the place from which John writes. Cp. v. 1 and notes.

III JOHN

1-4

We pass now to '"the Johannine Philemon", a private note concerned with personal relations'.[1]

Its similarity in form to that of everyday first-century private letters is notable. A papyrus letter[2] from Irenaeus, a ship's captain, to his brother Apolinarius makes this plain. It reads: 'Irenaeus to Apolinarius his brother, my greetings. Continually I pray that you may be in health, even as I myself am in health. I wish you to know that I arrived on land on the 6th of the month Epeiph. . . . (There follows his news of himself). . . . I greet your wife much, and Serenus, and all who love you, by name. Goodbye.' The pattern of III John is the same—the greeting: the prayer for good health: the central section with its main news: the final greetings 'by name'.

The letter is written by the Elder (v. 1), addressed to Gaius (v. 1), occasioned by Diotrephes (v. 9), and (probably) delivered by Demetrius (v. 12). See Introduction, pp. 139-143.

1. THE ELDER has been sufficiently discussed under II John 1; so also the likelihood that WHOM I LOVE IN THE TRUTH

---

[1] Aptly so described by A. M. Hunter, *Introducing the New Testament*, p. 180.

[2] Cited by Barclay, *The Letters of John*, p. 169. (See also Dodd, pp. 158 f.)

means more than ' whom I sincerely love ', signifying rather
' whom I love with that love which is the only fitting relation between us who are of the truth, i.e. between us
Christians.'

unto the well-beloved Gaius

A common Johannine epithet (ten times in the Epistles)
for a common name (e.g. Acts 19.29; 20.4; I Cor. 1.14).
Was this Gaius later made first bishop of Pergamum? The
Apostolic Constitutions says so, but it is a fourth-century
work of slight historical value.

The letter itself tells us Gaius is WELL-BELOVED (v. 1);
living a healthy Christian life (v. 2b); a ' child ' of John, i.e.
if not John's convert, at least pastorally dependent on him
(v. 4); well spoken of by the missionaries (THE BRETHREN,
vv. 3, 5, 10) to whom, it seems, he has already been host
(vv. 5 f.) and to whom he is encouraged to give future help
(vv. 6-8).

He emerges as a prominent member, with some influence
and means (see on BRING FORWARD, v. 6), in an Asian congregation; a man who, from past association and recent
news, can be trusted to align himself with the Elder in the
tensions made explicit in vv. 9-11. Is he layman or cleric?
We know not. Is he a member of the troubled congregation
or a neighbouring one? Verses 9-10 suggest Gaius is more
probably close to, but not of, the congregation of Diotrephes and his mischief.[1]

2. I wish above all things that thou mayest prosper

RSV turns the phrase neatly and more faithfully: ' I
pray that all may go well with you.' PROSPER translates
eu(h)odousthai, lit, ' have a good journey '. The RSV (and
NEB) ' go well ' is thus most apt.

---

[1] If this is to follow a false trail, then Gaius may be leader of the (? only
temporarily) minority party in the afflicted church.

even as thy soul prospereth

RSV: 'I know that it is well with your soul.' Tacked on
to the conventional PROSPER AND BE IN HEALTH, this clause
makes evident the supra-conventional level of the Elder's
concern for his correspondent. It sets the tone for the rest
of the letter. Note that Gaius' soul's health is not part of
the WISH or prayer of v. 2; it is known and stated as fact.
The evidence for the fact is adduced in vv. 3-6: the excellent
witness borne to Gaius' truth (v. 3) and love (v. 6), by
brethren reporting to John.

3. when the brethren came and testified . . .

Most naturally understood as reference to the BRETHREN
of vv. 5 and 10 and their testimony given BEFORE THE
CHURCH to Gaius' hospitality (v. 6).

thou walkest in the truth

i.e. lead a genuinely Christian life.

4. my children walk in truth

Gaius is by implication one of John's CHILDREN: possibly
his convert; more safely, his parishioner in the Asian diocese. John is his father-in-God. Gaius delights him because
Gaius fulfils the true pastor's supreme desire for all his
children: that they WALK IN TRUTH. Cp. II John 4.

THE HOST TO THE MISSIONARIES

5-8

This section treats of Gaius' relations with the 'brethren'. We call them 'missionaries' or 'missioners'. The
term 'missionaries' describes a body of men of great prestige in the early Church. Called 'prophets' by Paul, they
spent their lives—whole-time—in wandering, Spirit-led,

from place to place, preaching the word the Spirit gave them. The finest of them merited the special positions of respect the *Didache* makes plain they were given. Dr Barclay[1] cites *Did*. 10.7 in which, after the full Eucharist order has been detailed, and after the climactic prayer of thanksgiving has been set forth, there is the injunction: 'But suffer the prophets to give thanks as much as they will.'

The BRETHREN of this letter are such men: wandering prophets or missioners, with a regularly honoured place not in one congregation only but in any and all to which they were moved to travel.

Gaius is told that he 'does a loyal thing' (v. 5, RSV) (i.e. to the Church and the Elder) in rendering service to these men. John knows of Gaius' kindness to them because they had told of it in face of (presumably) John's own congregation (v. 6a). Now the brethren are back in the vicinity of Gaius, on another tour. Reasonable conjecture is that they have just come, with this letter borne by Demetrius their leader. John, counting on Gaius to repeat his former kindness, exhorts him to speed them worthily on their way (v. 6b). He commends the truly Christian purpose and high principle of these particular brethren. Thereby he underlines that Gaius' hospitality is alike their dire need and just desert (v. 7). John concludes the section: 'we are bound to support such men, and so play our part in spreading the truth' (v. 8, NEB).

5. whatsoever thou doest to the brethren, and to strangers

Misleading. The strangers *are* the brethren. Follow Dodd: 'Brethren, strangers as they are'. This makes Gaius' generosity the more notable. Unknown to him as they were, the itinerant missionaries had had his aid, simply as brothers-in-Christ in need of it.

[1] *Op. cit.*, p. 153.

6. bring forward on their journey

The verb, *propempein*, almost ' a technical term of Christian missions' (Dodd), means not merely 'speed someone on his way' but 'give financial help to someone for his journey.' Cp. Acts 15.3; 20.38; 21.5; I Cor. 16.6; Titus 3.13. See Dodd, p. 160 and in his *Romans*, on Rom. 15.24.

Gaius must have had the wherewithal, as well as the heart, to help.

after a godly sort

lit. worthily of God. RSV rightly translates: 'as befits God's service.'

7. for his name's sake

Cp. Acts 5.41. In this context the phrase emphasises the travellers' pure motivation. To proclaim Christ's name they have set out: for nothing else, nothing less. They *deserve* help in such disinterested and truth-advancing work. A contrast is implied with pagan wandering preachers who often made a great haul of money from their begging travels: a contrast, too, with heresy-spreading 'Christian' missionaries like those of I and II John. False and rascally 'Christian' itinerant prophets—abusing hospitality, 'trafficking in Christ' (*Christemporoi*)—were a great trial in the Church at the close of the first century. (See *Did*. 11 and 12, quoted by Barclay, p. 155.)

they went forth

Probably from John's church in Ephesus.

taking nothing of the Gentiles

Further ground for Gaius' support of them. In strict obedience to the spirit of our Lord's Mission Charge to the Twelve (Mark 6.8 f.; Matt. 10.9, etc.) these missionaries made no financial provision for their journey, trusting to receive hospitality as they went. Unlike others, they were most scrupulous to accept lodging and financial support only from Christian sources. By declining even 'contributions towards their expenses from well-disposed pagans' (Dodd), they kept themselves morally uncontaminated and kept their mission, even in appearance, uncompromised. As a result, they entirely depended on Gaius and Christians like him: those who, knowing the missionaries to be their fellow-Christians, would in brotherly love throw open their homes to the visitors and give generously for their support.

8. We therefore ought to receive such

Jews and Gentiles had long held hospitality to be a sacred duty. Christians, from earliest times, esteemed it as highly. Cp. I Peter 4.9; Heb. 13.2; Rom. 12.13; I Tim. 5.10; Titus 1.8. More than a general obligation to hospitality, however, is here expressed. (1) TO RECEIVE translates an inferior Greek text. The better, *hypolambanein*, 'suggests support as well as (hospitable) welcome' (Brooke). (2) It is SUCH, such admirable men as described in v. 7, to whom active support, as well as bed and board, is due.

fellow-helpers of the truth

RSV, 'fellow-workers in the truth'. Probably 'fellow-workers (with the missionaries) in the cause of the truth' is meant.

THE LETTER TO THE CHURCH

9a

I wrote unto the church

Lit. 'I wrote something (*ti*) to the church.' What is the something? Which church? Wrote about what? Intriguing questions defying certain answer. Can the 'something' be,

as several commentators in modern times suggest, our II
John? No ancient writer thought so. Further, THE CHURCH
here is, in the context of vv. 9b-10, most naturally that in
which Diotrephes is the leading offender. Now, if III John
had presented Diotrephes as a leading heretic on matters
of doctrine, we might believe the 'something' to be II John,
addressed, as that letter is, to a heresy-threatened church.
But in fact the Elder is silent on Diotrephes' doctrine.
(Strange if it were heretical!) His, and his church's, trouble
appears to be only indiscipline. Better, then, for us to see
in this 'something written to the church' a lost letter
addressed to Diotrephes' congregation concerning the 'missionary' matters dealt with in this letter to Gaius.

THE CHURCH, since unnamed, must have been well known
to Gaius. Was he a fellow-member of it, with Diotrephes?
By describing the details of the turmoil in the church as if
they were news to Gaius, vv. 9 f. suggest that Gaius was
not a member of it but, rather, a near neighbour, deeply
concerned.

THE LOVER OF PRE-EMINENCE

9b-11

This section, dominated by Diotrephes, poses two main
questions. (1) What were his misdeeds? and (2) What was
his ecclesiastical status?

(1) There are five counts against Diotrephes in the Elder's
eyes. He does not acknowledge the Elder's authority (RSV
for v. 9b). He talks malicious 'blethers' (*phlyarōn*) against
the Elder. He shuts his own door fast against the itinerant
missionaries come from the Elder. Worse: he makes this
private policy his church's policy. He prevents members
who are well-wishers of the missionaries from welcoming
and assisting them. Worst of all: he takes vengeance on the

opposition—these pro-missionary members—by excommunicating them.

Diotrephes' strength of personality is undoubted. Only a phenomenally strong man could have withstood the authority of the aged and widely revered ' disciple of the apostles ', talked actively against him, and put his hostility into drastic deeds. Only such a man could have roused the majority of the congregation to adopt his own rebellious position and to go so far as to sanction the excommunication of the minority. (That he had this majority following seems proved. Excommunication, even by a proper bishop, required popular concurrence. Further, if Diotrephes had only had minority support, the story would have been different. He would not have CAST OUT his opponents: he would have *walked* out, and, with his supporters, set up—like the heretics of I John—a separatist church.)

(2) The difficult, indeed insoluble, question is: Was this strength of personality joined to ecclesiastical authority earlier vested in him by the Church and exercised by him in the manner these verses describe? He behaves, certainly, like a bishop—that is, like a monarchical bishop, the single head of a local church, with a board of presbyters under him; just such a bishop as we find, early in the second century (in the Epistles of Ignatius, *c*. 115), in the various churches of this very province of Asia. Is Diotrephes in fact the duly appointed bishop of his church?

Our evidence is negligible and inconclusive. There is the apparently-promising term *philoprōteuōn* (v. 9b), WHO LOVETH TO HAVE THE PRE-EMINENCE, i.e. ' who likes to be first in everything '. But the word neither proves nor disproves his episcopacy. It expresses simply his ambitious love of power and top place.[1] Streeter[2] thought Diotrephes held this top place officially. Possibly so. Then Diotrephes is the

---

[1] NEB has ' their would-be leader '.
[2] *The Primitive Church*, Macmillan, 1929, pp. 83-89.

earliest known monarchical bishop—and one hostile to the
Elder John, the living link with the apostles.[1] But references
in Acts (20.17 f.) and in the Pastorals (Titus 1.5-9) (epistles
quite as late in date, perhaps, as III John) to the government
of the Asian churches speak only of boards of presbyters.
(Sometimes these are called 'bishops' but always they are
plural and synonymous with presbyters.) They are silent
about any single bishop governing any single church. This
fact rather cautions us against following Streeter. Besides,
would John not have been sure to attack any *Bishop* Diotrephes specifically for abuse of his episcopal *office*, especially if it were a recent innovation?

What then? Diotrephes perhaps was a layman who, by
great personal drive and agitation within the congregation,
made his will paramount and made himself a bishop not in
name but in effect. Possible, but a mighty jump for a layman! We rather see Diotrephes as neither layman nor
bishop but presbyter, a presbyter who forgot about being
inter pares! In this case, he so dominated and overrode his
colleagues in the kirk-session 'by force of character, or by
successful demagogy' (Dodd, p. 162) as to gain majority
support for shunning the Elder's missioners and excommunicating the minority.

Bishop? Layman? Presbyter? Diotrephes' ecclesiastical
status must, in the end, remain uncertain. Not so his viru-
lent antagonism to the Elder.

How are we to read the tension between John and Diotrephes? John may have thought that Diotrephes was,
through love of power, creating anarchy in his part of the
Asian 'diocese', the good order of which John regarded as
his responsibility. Diotrephes may have thought that John
—far away in Ephesus—was 'getting on' and 'getting past
it' and yet clinging to control of local congregations when
there were many able younger men (like Diotrephes) with

[1] The Elder's functions in the Asian group of churches would be those
of—at a later date—a metropolitan bishop, or archbishop.

their own, new, ideas (more related to the realities of the situation and the day) on how the Church, and their local church, should be run. Perhaps, in particular, Diotrephes thought that within his congregation or community (or both) these invasions by the Elder's missionaries were an embarrassment to that church's normal work, and should be banned, however painful the rupture with John, and within the church, might be.

No doubt blame belongs to both John and Diotrephes. 'Ageing men do not always yield with good grace an authority which under changed conditions they can no longer exercise effectively. Younger men, conscious of the growing needs and opportunities of a fresh generation, are not always considerate in grasping powers which are their due' (Dodd, p. 164). This lack of charity in Diotrephes, we may agree, makes his the greater blame in this unhappy episode. Ambitious lording it over others in the church, and excommunication of his opponents, bespeak his lovelessness. His treatment of the Elder himself is in keeping. Both men were foolish: Diotrephes was uncharitable and malicious as well, in deed as in words (PRATING AGAINST US WITH MALICIOUS WORDS).

So the final question Diotrephes presents is not 'Is he bishop, presbyter or layman?' but 'Is he Christian at all?' (See on v. 11, below.)

10. casteth them out of the church
The Greek could mean merely 'forcibly excludes them from the church meeting' or, even more mildly, '*tries* to expel them from the congregation'. Most natural, however, is the interpretation: 'excommunicates them from the Church'.

11. Gaius is urged to FOLLOW (Greek, 'imitate') THAT WHICH IS GOOD i.e. stay loyal to John and his missionary

policy. The EVIL he is to eschew is surely that of Diotrephes
in particular. Outwardly, it is the evil of defiant flouting of
the Elder's wishes; inwardly, as noted above, the evil of
lack of love. This truth about Diotrephes' motivation is the
key to the severe antithesis in v. 11b: HE THAT DOETH GOOD
IS OF GOD: BUT HE THAT DOETH EVIL HATH NOT SEEN GOD.
We recall that in I John 'doing good' or 'being of God'
means primarily the practice of love (see I John 2.7-11;
2.3-5; 2.29-3.1; 3.4-10; 4.7-12 and notes, for meaning of 'of
God' and 'seeing God'). Diotrephes' failure in love stamps
him as one who has NOT SEEN GOD. He is no Christian: still
less, we may add, one fit to have 'the pre-eminence among
them'.

Now John swiftly turns Gaius' eyes right away from the
evil example, to Demetrius (v. 12), one who embodies that
good which the Elder exhorts Gaius to imitate.

THE EMBODIMENT OF THE TRUTH

12

All we know of Demetrius is in this single verse.[1] The
picture is vivid, nonetheless, of a man of model Christian
faith and practice. His position we can only guess, but some
guesses are better than others. He could be a member in the
congregation of Diotrephes, or that of Gaius; singled out
by the Elder as someone Gaius may absolutely trust in the
tensions of the time. More probably Demetrius was one of,
even leader of, the group of missionaries to visit Gaius and
was entrusted with the delivery of this letter to Gaius. Verse
12 then becomes an introductory 'reference', or testimonial,
to the worth of Demetrius. Such testimonials were common
and understandably important in the difficult and dangerous

[1] The *Apostolic Constitutions,* too late to be good evidence, says John
made him Bishop of Philadelphia.

days of the early Church. Cp. Rom. 16.12; Col. 4.7-8. Interesting allusion is made to these 'certificates' (Moffatt) in II Cor. 3.1: 'Need we, as some others, epistles of commendation to you, or letters of commendation from you?'

What is said of Demetrius? Threefold witness is given to his excellence: that of ALL MEN, that of THE TRUTH ITSELF, and that of the Elder (the WE of v. 12b) personally. (For the compelling power of conjoint witness cp. I John 5.6 ff., and notes.)

of all

All acquainted with Demetrius in his church and the Church at large. 'Everybody testifies to Demetrius' (Moffatt) suggests both widespread knowledge of him and unanimously high regard.

of the truth itself

This unusual phrase could mean simply: 'the unanimously good opinion about Demetrius is more than opinion: it is the plain truth about him.' Brooke, however, would personify THE TRUTH here and identify it with Christ or the Holy Spirit, yielding the sense 'The Truth itself (i.e. Christ or Holy Spirit) also testifies to Demetrius.' Best of all is to take THE TRUTH as *not* personified but in the sense, and relations, studied in e.g. I John 1.6; 3.18-19; II John 4; III John 4. The meaning then is: 'Demetrius' way of life is such (i.e. his consistency in loving practice is such) that he is plainly seen to be " walking in the truth "; so ideally does he realise this Christian requirement that the truth itself shines out of him and "speaks for him " in all he does.'

This witness of THE TRUTH ITSELF to Demetrius—this 'self-evidencing integrity of his life' (Dodd)—might well be thought ample record to satisfy Gaius, especially when prefaced by the witness of general esteem. John knows Gaius well, however. He realises that the most immediately potent word to Gaius in Demetrius' favour is the one John can speak on his own account. So he puts down—last—his personal testimony.

Yea, and we also bear record

It has the weight not only of his position in the Church but of all that over the years Gaius has found the Elder to be. He can say: 'Thou knowest (better reading than AV YE KNOW) 'that our record is true.' (Cp. John 21.24.) In effectiveness the Elder's own, his final witness to Demetrius, would prove a true climax.

FINAL GREETINGS

13-14

Except for its PEN (lit. reed) in place of 'paper', its SHORTLY SEE THEE instead of 'come unto you', and its lack of the phrase 'that our joy may be full', the epistolary formula of vv. 13-14a (. . . FACE TO FACE) repeats that of II John 12. See notes thereon. The differences are without significance.

13. I had many things to write

As in II John 12, this may be a familiar epistolary fiction, as practised in every age! Conceivably, however, John may have had abundance to write but now felt that he had exhausted writing's usefulness in the delicate state of church affairs adumbrated in the letter. The rest could only be done, wisely and effectively, FACE TO FACE (lit. mouth to mouth; cp. II John 12) with Gaius. This he hopes to do soon.

14b. Peace be to thee

Cp. I Peter 5.14; John 14.27. The normal Jewish greeting,

taken over by Christians. Yet the phrase has a special appositeness in the setting of this epistle, and in the personal need of Gaius and his like-minded brethren.

The remaining phrases are both in regular first-century letter form. Note that in the more formal, pastoral II John the greetings are from the church members *en masse*; here they are private greetings, befitting a private letter: OUR (lit. the) FRIENDS SALUTE THEE. Finally Gaius is told:

Greet the friends by name

'one by one' (Moffatt); 'individually' (NEB). Both AV and Moffatt have led some to the erroneous conclusion that the circle of Gaius' pro-Presbyter friends must have been tiny enough for this 'one by one' greeting to be literally carried out! The phrase BY NAME is in fact standard usage in letters of the time. Cp. e.g. Oxyrhynchus Papyri I.123: 'I greet my dearest daughter Makkaria and my lady your mother and all our folks by name.'

Dodd's comment could not be bettered. The Elder's intention 'is simply to individualise for the recipients a courtesy which in writing must needs be left general.'

For Reference

Not to be taken from this room